To G.

With best ?

Gareth David

November 2023

CROYDON TRAMLINK

In memory of Stephen Parascandalo (1980-2007)

Tramlink's No. 1 enthusiast

At his 2003 Brunel University graduation ceremony, Stephen Parascandalo
stands alongside a boyhood hero, Isambard Kingdom Brunel.

FRONT COVER: Two generations of tram at Mitcham on 31 October 2018, where Stadler 2562 on a Wimbledon service passes
Bombardier 2535 bound for Elmers End.

REAR COVER: A pleasantly rural scene at Lloyd Park on 28 January 2019, where 2534 has just left the stop with a
New Addington–West Croydon service.

Sunshine and snow as 2547 comes off the Beckenham Junction line at Arena with a service for West Croydon.

Stadler trams 2564 and 2554 (in purple 'Love Croydon' livery) await attention inside Therapia Lane depot on 16 January 2019.

CROYDON TRAMLINK

A DEFINITIVE HISTORY

GARETH DAVID

PEN & SWORD
TRANSPORT

AN IMPRINT OF PEN & SWORD BOOKS LTD.
YORKSHIRE - PHILADELPHIA

First published in Great Britain in 2020 by
Pen and Sword Transport
An imprint of
Pen & Sword Books Ltd
Yorkshire - Philadelphia

ISBN 978 1 52671 953 9

A CIP catalogue record for this book is available from the British Library.

Typeset by Aura Technology and Software Services, India.
Printed and bound in India by Replika Press Pvt. Ltd.

Pen & Sword Books Ltd incorporates the Imprints of Pen & Sword Books Archaeology, Atlas, Aviation, Battleground, Discovery, Family History, History, Maritime, Military, Naval, Politics, Railways, Select, Transport, True Crime, Fiction, Frontline Books, Leo Cooper, Praetorian Press, Seaforth Publishing, Wharncliffe and White Owl.

For a complete list of Pen & Sword titles please contact

PEN & SWORD BOOKS LIMITED
47 Church Street, Barnsley, South Yorkshire, S70 2AS, England
E-mail: enquiries@pen-and-sword.co.uk
Website: www.pen-and-sword.co.uk

or

PEN AND SWORD BOOKS
1950 Lawrence Rd, Havertown, PA 19083, USA
E-mail: Uspen-and-sword@casematepublishers.com
Website: www.penandswordbooks.com

CONTENTS

THE AUTHOR

Gareth David developed a life-long interest in railways and public transport while growing up in Cheltenham Spa during the 1960s and early 1970s, then moved to London, where he read Modern History at University College (UCL). On graduating in 1979 he trained as a journalist, before joining The Times as Stock Market Reporter in early 1982. He went on to work on the business section of The Observer and later The Sunday Times, where he was Deputy City Editor from 1988-90.

A highlight of his subsequent career in public relations consultancy was to support Ian Yeowart for twelve years in battling to launch 'Open Access' operator Grand Central Railway Company. Gareth now lives at Haslemere in Surrey and was a daily commuter to London Waterloo for twenty-five years. He is married to Clare and has four grown-up children. In his spare time Gareth works as a volunteer booking clerk or buffet car steward on the Mid-Hants Railway (Watercress Line).

His first book, Railway Renaissance, was published by Pen & Sword in September 2017 and his second, Britain's last mechanical signalling, in June 2019. To learn more, please visit www.railwayworld.net.

FOREWORD

To my surprise, I realise I have been involved with, and interested in, trams in and around Croydon for almost seventy years. I have a clear memory of riding with my mother on one of the originals in South Croydon just before they were withdrawn in 1951.

In the late 1990s, I helped push the first of the new generation of Light Rail Vehicles into Therapia Lane depot after it had come off a low loader. To my great pride, I was asked to be 'the voice of the Croydon tram'. So it is my on-board announcements passengers have heard for the past two decades.

It is a great pleasure to write a short introduction to this new and detailed study of a system which remains into the foreseeable future London's only modern tram system. The achievements have been many, the travelling habits of so many people have been changed and massively improved, and there must be some hope that much-needed extensions will be built.

I pay tribute to Gareth David's painstaking research. He has managed to talk to just about every important person involved in the system's development, to learn about the very earliest ideas and how the route layouts were settled.

There is quite rightly a lengthy examination of the dreadful accident at Sandilands in 2016. From tragedy has come new ways of ensuring safer

Nicholas Owen, former ITN newsreader and the 'Voice of Tramlink'.

operation of tramcars in the UK in the future.

I am sure this book will be of great interest to anyone who knows what most local people still think of as the Croydon Trams. Let us hope that the full and fascinating story of what is now officially called London Tramlink will encourage the spread of light rail systems elsewhere.

NICHOLAS OWEN

INTRODUCTION

Light rail has been one of the major success stories in UK public transport over the past two decades, with developments in places such as Birmingham, Nottingham, Sheffield, Edinburgh and continued expansion in Manchester, so it is perhaps hard today to appreciate the true significance of Tramlink.

When it opened in May 2000 it brought trams back onto the streets of London for the first time in almost half a century – to be precise, since the early hours of 6 July 1952, when car no. 1951 entered New Cross tram depot and ended the capital's love affair with what Americans aptly call the streetcar.

Croydon had lost its last trams just over a year before that fateful night in New Cross when, on 7 April 1951, services had ended on its final three routes, 16/18 (Purley–Embankment) and 42 (Croydon–Thornton Heath). Yet only a year earlier, the concept of what is now a principal Tramlink route was first suggested, when the Mayor of Croydon proposed running trams from East Croydon station to the major new post-war housing estate being built east of the town at New Addington.

The rationale here was that many of London Transport's most modern 'Feltham' tramcars were being moved to Leeds (operating there until 1959), where they would serve new housing developments using reserved tracks. Nothing, alas, came of this far-sighted initiative, and it would be exactly fifty years and the year 2000 when the residents of New Addington would finally be able to board a tramcar bound for Croydon.

As detailed in the following chapters, studies into the development of Tramlink began in the late 1980s, as a means of tackling the growing issue of traffic congestion and of accessibility to the town centre from New Addington in particular. What was launched, slightly behind schedule, on 10 May 2000, was a 17.5-mile (28.2km) system, with 38 stops (since increased to 39), linking central Croydon and East Croydon station on four routes with New Addington, Beckenham, Elmers End and Wimbledon.

Much of the system uses former railway lines, with a limited amount of street running through the centre of Croydon, and continental-style segregated track on much of the New Addington route.

After a somewhat hesitant beginning, and initial numbers falling short of the forecasts and financial needs of Tramlink's private sector owners/operators, a radical change to the fares regime and later a takeover by Transport for London in 2008 has seen Tramlink live up to, and then exceed, all expectations.

Passenger numbers have risen from 18.2 million in its first full year of operation (2001/2) to 29.1 million in 2017/8 and are forecast to rise still further to 60 million by 2030. That growth has already seen the initial 24-strong tram fleet increased in size by 12 and the initial infrastructure enhanced with additional sections of double track to increase the system's capacity.

Tramlink has become a victim of its own success, and as the system celebrates its 20th anniversary, major investment decisions will have to be taken in the near future regarding system expansion and further new vehicles if it is to cope with the anticipated level of further growth in passenger numbers.

The Tramlink story is essentially about how one corner of Greater London identified, and then created, an environmentally-friendly and sustainable solution to its urgent need for improved local transport. As the following chapters will illustrate, it is a tale full of colour, incident and, on one fateful occasion, tragedy.

GLOSSARY & DRAMATIS PERSONAE

David Bayliss
A former Director of Planning at London Transport

Bombardier
Member of the TCL consortium, supplier of the 24-strong fleet of CR4000 tram vehicles

Peter (now Lord) Bowness
Leader of Croydon Council 1980-84

British Rail (BR)
Nationalised UK railway network owner and operator until privatisation in 1996

Bus Rapid Transit (BRT)
Bus-based public transport system, featuring dedicated bus lanes

Centrewest
Former London Buses subsidiary, and member of the TCL consortium

Concession Agreement
99-year legal agreement (from 1996) under which TCL built and operates Tramlink

David Congdon
MP for Croydon North East (Conservative) and sponsor of the Croydon Tramlink Bill

Dennis Coombes
A former Director of Highways & Transportation at Croydon Council

CR4000
Design of the initial 24-strong tram fleet supplied by Bombardier (2530-2553)

Croydon Advertiser
Principal local newspaper in Croydon area

Croydon Council
The London Borough of Croydon – promoter of Tramlink

Croydon Tramlink Bill (Act)
Parliamentary legislation enabling construction and funding of Tramlink

Paul Davison
Managing Director of TCL at the time of its 2008 buy-out by TfL

Nico Dekker
Independent consultant working for LT on development of Tramlink

Design, Build, Finance & Operate (DBFO)
Government mechanism for the funding and delivery of infrastructure projects

Docklands Light Railway (DLR)
London's first light rail system – opened in 1987 and since significantly expanded

Bob Dorey OBE
Chairman of TCL at the time Tramlink opened. Died in 2018 (aged 78)

FirstGroup
UK bus and rail operator – owner of Tram Operations Ltd

GEC Alstom Transportation Projects (GEC)
Consultancy which produced independent report on development of Tramlink

Greater London Authority (GLA)
Regional governance body for London, established in 2000

Roger Harding
A former General Manager of TCL

(Sir) Peter Hendy
Led buy-out of Centrewest from London Buses, later TfL Transport Commissioner

Phil Hewitt
A former Head of Trams at TfL, now Managing Director of Midland Metro

Halcrow Fox (HFA)
Consultancy which produced Tramlink's Environmental Statement

Her Majesty's Railway Inspectorate (HMRI)
Body responsible for overseeing safety on Britain's railways and tramways

Improvement Notice
Safety recommendation(s) made following an RAIB investigation

Boris Johnson
Mayor of London from May 2008 until May 2016

Light Rapid Transit
Generic name given to urban public transport developments such as Tramlink

Ken Livingstone
First Mayor of London (May 2000-May 2008)

Scott McIntosh
Former Director of Light Rail at LT and closely involved with development of Tramlink

Piers Merchant MP
Conservative MP for Beckenham 1992-97 and leading opponent of Tramlink

Midland Metro
Tram network based on Birmingham, developed at same time as Tramlink

Steve(n) Norris MP
A former Minister of Transport for London

Office of Rail and Road (ORR)
Regulatory body, known until April 2015 as the Office of Rail Regulation

Private Finance Initiative (PFI)
Mechanism for using private sector funding to deliver infrastructure projects

Project Development Group (PDG)
Consortium (Tarmac, AEG, Transdev) formed to develop specification for Tramlink

Rail Accident Investigation Branch (RAIB)
Independent body investigating incidents on Britain's railways and tramways

Road Traffic Accident (RTA)
Incident involving a motor vehicle

John Rymer
Managing Director of Tram Operations Ltd until September 2017

Jim Snowdon
A former Engineering Manager at TCL

London Buses Limited
Formed in 1985 to manage London's buses – now a subsidiary of TfL

London Regional Transport
Controlled London Transport 1984-2000 and since replaced by TfL

Stadler
Swiss manufacturer of the latest twelve Variobahn tram vehicles (2554-2565)

Jackie Townsend
Managing Director of Tram Operations Ltd (TOL) since September 2017

Transport Act (1968) – Section 56
Provision for Government to support capital expenditure on public transport projects

Transport for London (TfL)
Created in 2000 as successor to London
Regional Transport

Tram Operations Limited (TOL)
A wholly-owned subsidiary of FirstGroup
and operator of Tramlink since 2000

Tramtrack Croydon Limited (TCL)
Company (consortium) selected to build
and run Tramlink – owned since 2008 by TfL

Transdev
French-owned public transport operator
formerly active in London

Travelcard
Zonal fares scheme covering all rail/bus/
tram networks in Greater London

Turner & Townsend (T&T)
Consultancy firm providing advice during
the construction of Tramlink

Variobahn
Design name for the twelve-strong fleet of
trams supplied by Stadler (2554-2565)

CHAPTER 1

THE OPPORTUNITY IN CROYDON

Crucial to the viability of Tramlink was the opportunity to make use of two British Rail routes, one of which had closed shortly before the first light rail studies (Elmers End to Sanderstead in 1983) and one an under-utilised corridor with a lightly-used passenger service linking two important centres (Croydon and Wimbledon) and having significant potential for development.

Another key driver was the pressing need to improve links between the town centre and New Addington, a residential development on the east side of Croydon, first started in the 1930s but expanded in the post-war years to become a settlement of around 25,000 people. Its links to Croydon were totally inadequate, with bus services taking up to 45 minutes to reach East Croydon at peak times, a distance of just 5 miles.

Croydon had grown rapidly in the nineteenth century, and was very congested in the centre of the town and had a lot of very sub-standard property. A solution to that had been the creation of New Addington, which was originally started by a charity, the Croydon Sanitary Housing Association, and built on a similar philosophy to post-war new towns such as Basildon – as a town, not a dormitory suburb, so it was built in fields some distance, but not too far, from Croydon.

Just as Basildon New Town in Essex did not get a railway station at the outset, because it would simply have encouraged people to go and work in London, the idea was that there were going to be factories around New Addington, so people would live and work there and maybe once a week would hop on a bus and go into Croydon for their big shopping trip and to visit department stores. Essentially it was to be self-contained.

But that never happened. Once decent houses have been built, they fill up with people who want to commute to somewhere better. In the case of Croydon that meant new, thriving industries like the Pye electronics factory, the Payne's sweets factory and others which grew up along Purley Way to the west of Croydon, which became an early (1920s) example of a by-pass road attracting strip development along it.

Further out in the same direction was the Wandle Valley, which had a lot of industrial employment. It was started just before the Second World War, then went into suspense during the war, before building and expansion resumed. So most people living in New Addington needed to either get to Croydon or beyond Croydon to the other side of the town to Purley Way and the Wandle Valley.

Croydon had also suffered significant damage during the war. Being on the last hill before you get into London, German 'doodlebugs' would be running out of power by the time they got to Croydon, so there was some quite significant bomb damage during the 1940s, giving post-war Croydon the ethos of a new town as its central area was rebuilt.

Legacies of that post-war rebuilding include the notorious Croydon underpass – a six-lane highway running north to south through the central area, now regarded as a rather foolish piece of road-based planning. At the same time, Croydon saw construction of numerous office blocks in the early 1950s under the Government's dispersal of offices programme – places such as Lunar House, home to the Department for Immigration.

By the 1980s the problem facing Croydon was that, with London Docklands starting to take off, these office blocks were not as attractive as they had once been. Croydon Council, being a business-orientated body, commissioned research which indicated that, if left as they were, rents would fall, the quality and length of tenancies would fall, and the town would slip into decline relative to competing parts of London, and Docklands in particular.

So Croydon had to decide what it was going to do to address these two pressing issues, with New Addington poorly served by public transport, while there was a vital need to rejuvenate the town centre at a time when traffic problems were increasing. Added to that, the Wandle Valley was in terminal decline in terms of employment, and was likely to be redeveloped with housing, so how were its new residents going to get into Croydon to shop and to access the commuter railway stations at East or West Croydon?

These were the early days of Thameslink, and it had not yet reached East Croydon, but there was a train every three or four minutes from East Croydon to Central London, taking just 17 minutes. At the western end of the Wandle Valley, Wimbledon had trains to Central London every couple of minutes, so the challenge was to look at ways to link the two, as well as address the New Addington issue, and Croydon Council realised that a roads-based policy was not going to succeed.

The Council looked at how much road widening or road improvement would be necessary to carry the traffic which Croydon was predicted to have, but realised that it was going to be politically impossible to deliver. People in their nice 1930s houses were simply not going to accept losing their front gardens completely. So it was a case of how do you come up with a solution that improves connectivity but also helps to make the borough a more attractive place.

Early studies

Addressing the New Addington challenge meant that in the 1960s, 70s, and early 80s a whole raft of weird and wonderful solutions had been put forward to solve its transport issues, including monorails, hover-trains and computer-controlled mini-trams. One that caught a few people's attention was a monorail, but that would have meant seeing trains travelling three or four metres above ground and passing through Shirley Woods, which is a site of outstanding natural beauty and a Site of Special Scientific Interest (SSSI), so it was never going to be too popular.

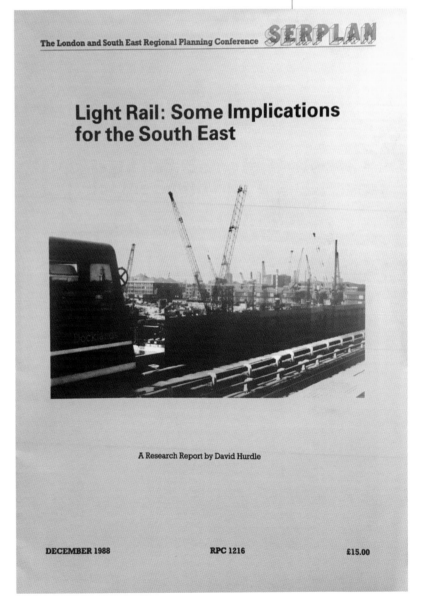

One of the earliest studies into the potential for light rail in Croydon.

The London and South East Regional Planning Conference **SERPLAN**

Light Rail: Some Implications for the South East

A Research Report by David Hurdle

DECEMBER 1988   RPC 1216   £15.00

As early as 1962 a private study, with assistance from BR engineers, showed how easy it was to convert the West Croydon-Wimbledon route to tram operation and successfully prevent conflict between trams and trains. During the 1970s, several BR directors and managers were aware of the advantages, and Chris Green, Managing Director of BR's Network SouthEast sector, published plans in 1987 for expanding the concept to take in the Tattenham Corner and Caterham branches and provide a service from Croydon to Lewisham via Addiscombe and Hayes.

Scott McIntosh, a former Director of Light Rail at London Transport (LT) and someone closely involved in Tramlink's early development, recalls how his predecessor, Tim Runnacles, had undertaken a number of studies that had been submitted to LT. 'He had looked at the Oxford Street problem and had looked at New Addington and had suggested way back in the 1970s that one sensible solution would be an electric tramway. He even had sketches of what looked like a pair of Leyland 'Atlantean' buses on wheels – double deck ones at that – so there were ideas going around!'

Light rail as a solution to Croydon's transport needs was first formally identified in a study called *Light Rail for London*, which was produced jointly by London Transport and British Rail in 1986. This looked at the scope for converting existing or disused railway lines to light rail, and noted that Croydon – where there were a number of closed or lightly-used rail alignments – could provide the focus for one of the most promising networks.

The following year (1987) a Light Rail study – again by LT/BR, but with the involvement of officers from Croydon Council – concluded that an initial network, comprising three lines from central Croydon to Wimbledon, Elmers End and New Addington, appeared to be feasible from engineering, environmental and economic viewpoints, and should be investigated more fully.

While ideas about a light rail solution to Croydon's transport needs were evolving, work known as the London Assessment Studies was looking at wider transport issues in a number of key corridors across the capital, including the A23 at Croydon. Options for improvements were published in 1988, featuring both better public transport and road improvements, with three recommended options all incorporating a light rail system, though somewhat larger in scope than what was ultimately developed as Tramlink. Proposed road improvements aroused considerable opposition and were abandoned, but in its response to a public consultation exercise, the Department of Transport endorsed the principle of a light rail solution in Croydon.

Financial constraints

A running theme in London's public transport from the post-war period of the late 1940s until the 1980s was shortage of funds for maintaining and developing the various networks, never mind the huge capital cost of expansion. Governments after the war showed a marked reluctance to commit huge sums into London Underground (LU), which by the early 1980s had become more seriously run-down than many people cared to admit, with ageing rolling stock and escalators, as was tragically exposed in the King's Cross fire of 1987.

While the last trams in the capital had run in 1952, a decade later the last trolley buses ran (1962), because London Buses did not want to put any investment in a new fleet. That was good news for cash-starved LU however, because it was able to acquire Greenwich Power Station, which had been a London County Council tramway power station providing electricity for the South London tramways and trolley bus networks.

London Buses, meanwhile, continued to roughly break even in the 1970s and early 1980s, recording a pattern of gently declining ridership that has been the history of UK buses since the Second World War. So anyone suggesting expenditure on something new – like a light rail system – was not likely to be greeted with glowing warmth by LU management, who felt that anything spent on a new project was taking what they believed was their money.

That was one of the reasons why the Docklands Light Railway (DLR) and its promoters within LT and the London Docklands Development Corporation (LDDC) did a deal with Margaret Thatcher's Government to secure a ring-fenced sum of £77 million to develop the initial DLR network. The fact that the DLR was hopelessly under-specified at the outset, spurring on a succession of ever grander office developments along its route through the Isle of Dogs, showed how an area could just take off, given decent accessibility.

A key appointment at LT

The driving force behind development of Tramlink within LT was Scott McIntosh, a no-nonsense law graduate, who had begun his career in the Royal Navy, where he had studied marine engineering at the Britannia Naval College in Dartmouth. McIntosh had been involved in preserved railways from an early age, including the tramway museum at Crich in Derbyshire, so was not afraid of working on live overhead wires and, crucially, had a real passion for the subject of light rail.

Having left the Royal Navy and moved to London, his first introduction to the transport scene came on the DLR, where he secured a temporary role in testing the passenger vehicles as they were delivered in the two years before the system opening. It was a role where he faced some significant challenges in proving the electric circuitry in every car that was delivered, even challenging the German manufacturers by telling them that the traction motors were wired the wrong way

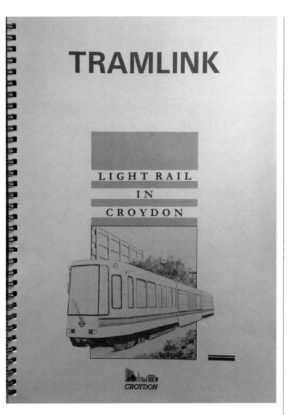

An early consultation document, published by Croydon Council in April 1991.

round, a move which secured him a full-time role!

McIntosh recalls some of the early challenges he faced, with the new automated trains stopping all over the place: 'I remember going on holiday and talking to the chief operations manager of Bay Area Rapid Transit in San Francisco [the only other automated metro in the world at the time] and saying to him that we kept having trains which thought they had got to the next station, find they haven't docked in [found docking coils at the station] and so they just switch off. He told me that I was lucky and that he had trains coming through the 3.5 mile long Trans-Bay tunnel at 60 mph, that don't find the station and go straight through the platform at full speed!'

McIntosh spent three years on the DLR before being head-hunted to join London Underground, where his first boss was a Polish man called Mike Strzelecki, who was undertaking a project called the reorganisation of London Underground, which involved the setting up of a line-management structure. In 1988 he moved into the planning department at LT, which was led by a well-respected director named David Bayliss, who had started work as a tram 'clippie' in Blackpool during university vacations.

This was the height of the Thatcher era and LT was desperate not to have people breaking up the tube system, so Bayliss was kept very busy dealing with the new Jubilee Line extension and a plan by Docklands developer G. Ware Travelsted, who wanted to build a private tube line from Canary Wharf to Waterloo. Bayliss left McIntosh to work up plans for Tramlink, instructing him not to spend any money out of the budget over and above what he had been given.

'I arrived literally to an office with a telephone, and a single sheet of paper, which said we need to develop a new innovative scheme to provide public transport in Croydon, so that's what I did,' recalls McIntosh. 'The history of LT is that it tended to tell London boroughs what it was going to do and they would just salute and do what they were told. That was alright when dealing with smaller boroughs, but there had been the re-organisation of London boroughs by then, and we had this population of one-third of a million south of London, which thought of itself as a city.

'I thought that this was going to be absolutely awful, because I have to keep this project on the go, and the problem was that Croydon Council had a Department of Highways and Transportation. Of course they knew nothing about public transport; all they knew about was roads, because that is all they had been allowed to play with for the past 50 years. They knew very little about railways, very little about buses and nothing about trams, so this looked like it was going to be hell!'

Working with Croydon Council

One key working relationship for McIntosh was with Dennis Coombes, Croydon Council's Director of Highways and Transportation, and it was the strength of that relationship which laid the groundwork for a constructive partnership that, twelve years later, would deliver the Tramlink network as it is today.

'I used to go and see Dennis in his office and the meetings would go on for hours and hours and hours,' recalls McIntosh. 'I would come out feeling like I had been sucked dry of every bit of information I had, but I was a bit careful, because I thought that if we gave them too much information, they would think they know it all, and then they could go along to the Tory Government and say we can do all this ourselves, we don't need LT.

'Dennis used to invite me to turn up to his office at about 3.30–4.00pm. It took me some time to realise that Dennis was a chain smoker and staff were not allowed to smoke in their offices, but after 5.30pm everybody had gone home, so Dennis would look at his watch, open the big cigarette box on his desk and begin chain smoking. There were some nights I did not get home until 11.00pm, we would just go on and on and he would want to know the ins and outs of everything.

'I very quickly realised that Dennis had his department very well in hand – everybody respected him and he did not have to shout to get what he wanted done. Councillors were very appreciative of what he did, and did something very sensible by setting up a committee of five – three from the majority (Conservative) party, two from the minority party and the leader of the Council would be one of the members and would chair it.

'That was great, because when Croydon turned from being a Tory Council to a Labour Council, all that happened was that one Councillor stepped down from the committee and another stepped in, so the committee carried on and we had continuity. The great thing was that the Labour Councillors were what I would call 'Old Labour' – concerned about what it would do for their people in New Addington, not the revolution! So, as long

A document sent to prospective tenderers for the PFI contract.

as you could talk to them in a sensible way, it was fine.

'I can remember one meeting where one of these people raised a problem about a right turn out of a street that came onto the Croydon under-pass [Wellesley Road] – and what if something went wrong here. It was Peter [now Lord] Bowness, who was very suave, was sitting there and after two or three minutes he has really had enough of anything technical and said: "I think that if Mr Coombes says it will be alright, then we don't need to worry. Mr Coombes, will it be alright?"

"Yes leader," replied Coombes.

'When we had a break, I said to Dennis that we haven't even discussed this problem. He said, "yes, I know, but we'll find a solution". Dennis was clever and always wore Marks & Spencer suits – he said it is a Tory Council and they expect their senior officers to wear suits, but if I wore a tailored suit, they would think they are paying me too much!

'We formed a body called the Tramlink Liaison Committee and offered a seat on it to Merton Council, but they refused, and their view was that we are not having any trams in Merton. We will tolerate you converting the technology on the West Croydon–Wimbledon railway line, but after that we don't want to know and besides, we want to make your life absolute hell until somebody does something about major grade segregation on the A3 where it crosses the railway line. They were not co-operative at all.'

Following Coombes' death from cancer on 3 July 2002, McIntosh wrote a glowing tribute to the part the former Director of Highways and Transportation at the London Borough of Croydon had played in the delivery of Tramlink: 'He worked tirelessly for the introduction of Tramlink, helping to find solutions to many of the problems that seemed to stand in the way. He led a multi-disciplinary team of council officers with skill and enthusiasm. Without his help London Transport would have found the introduction of Tramlink almost impossible… With his death Tramlink has lost one of its parents, the industry has lost significant expertise and I have lost a friend and colleague for whom I had the greatest respect.'

Crucial deals with British Rail

At the same time as he was forging good working relationships with Croydon Council, McIntosh also formed a working group with a team at British Rail. BR had a problem with the Wimbledon–West Croydon line. At the Wimbledon end it went into Wimbledon station, but it shared a platform with what are now the Thameslink services. In many places the line may have looked like it was double track, but actually never had been – it had always been one passenger line and a series of freight loops giving access to the different industrial sites including Croydon A&B power stations.

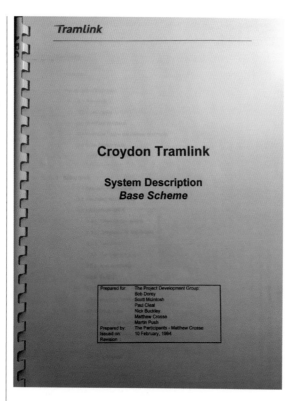

All of these industrial users had since gone and the rail infrastructure was very old. Some of it dated back to the Surrey Iron Railway in the early nineteenth century, the stations were run-down, and it could only handle two-car trains because the bay platform at West Croydon was very short. To make matters even more urgent, there would not be any two-car trains available when the 'slam door' 2 EPB units used on the route were finally withdrawn. It had also been electrified on the cheap in the 1920s, so by the late 1980s was in a bad way.

McIntosh recalls the ease with which he was able to acquire this crucial alignment for the future Tramlink: 'The prospect of somebody taking this line over was greeted with open arms by BR, so eventually we bought the line for £1.00 – that's the advantage when it's two nationalised industries, you can just swop things around!

'On the other side of town, we were fortunate that BR owned the remains of the South Croydon Line [Elmers End–Selsdon], which had the three tunnels that would take us under the more sensitive

parts of Croydon. The track had been lifted, but BR still owned the trackbed and had the maintenance liabilities, so was quite happy to get rid of that as well. BR also offered us the Elmers End–Addiscombe branch line, because again it wanted to get rid of Addiscombe and had already received offers for the station site from housing developers, as it was quite a big site.'

Getting to Beckenham Junction

Under its original plans, Tramlink would have terminated at Elmers End station, where it made a connection with BR services on the route from London Charing Cross and Cannon Street to Hayes. But McIntosh was not happy, saying that Elmers End is nowhere, and there would be no significant traffic originating there.

Instead he looked at running the new light rail system out of Elmers End station, up Elmers End Road and Croydon Road into the centre of Elmers End, where there was a triangle of land and space for a terminus. Local buses all serve this point, so services could have been reorganised to act as feeders to the tram. But London Buses was not enthusiastic about that idea and, from an engineering point of view, it would have been very difficult because Elmers End station is below the level of the road and getting out of the station and up onto the road bridge would have been difficult.

Realising the limitations of Elmers End, McIntosh looked at running trams to Beckenham Junction, not for the sake of going to Beckenham Junction, but because between Croydon Arena and Beckenham Junction the railway was lined with street after street of late Victorian terraced houses, the larger ones having been split into two flats and the smaller ones being three-bed houses. That meant fertile commuter territory and a great market for public transport. So evolved the idea of building a branch off the Elmers End line, running past Croydon Arena and in

CROYDON COUNCIL AND LONDON TRANSPORT

CROYDON TRAMLINK

ENVIRONMENTAL STATEMENT

HFA

Halcrow Fox and Associates
Vineyard House
44 Brook Green
London W6 7BY

The all-important Environmental Statement, published in November 1991.

a rising spiral to become a single track alongside the railway into Beckenham Junction.

'Amazingly, we never put it to the LT Board and it never went to the BR regional board, it was just a quiet agreement, an exchange of emails between two officers at LT and BR that we would take over the line to Beckenham Junction. The only thing BR said was that under no circumstances whatsoever do you get within a metre of the telephone exchange or the cable ducts out of it at Beckenham Junction, because if you do the whole of London Bridge signal box or something similar closes down!

'So we had to create an awkward entry to the station, which was quite fortunate in one way because it led us to develop our approach to terminal stations of pulling two tracks into one and then spreading one track out to two, meaning all of the stations could accept and despatch trains from both platforms and all you had were two plain standard turn-outs [sets of points], instead of needing scissors

cross-overs. That concept all started because we had to have only a single line to Beckenham Junction.'

Confirming the need for Tramlink

Further endorsement of a light rail solution to Croydon's transport needs came in a research report, 'Light Rail: Some Implications for the South East', written by David Hurdle for the London and South East Regional Planning Conference (Serplan) and published in December 1988. Serplan is a body made up of every local authority across South-East England and this report was published at a time when Croydon was one of more than thirty proposals for light rail schemes across the UK, of which the only other schemes to actually come to fruition were those in Edinburgh and Nottingham, along with further extensions to Manchester's existing Metrolink network.

In referring to Croydon, Hurdle noted (para 4.15), 'Croydon town centre is the largest shopping area in the region outside Central London and is the country's sixth largest office location... A LR system comprising converted BR lines, a new link between the two town centre stations and a new route to New Addington, a residential area of 30,000 people 8km away unserved by rail, would markedly increase accessibility and could transfer trips from car to rail... A significant operating surplus would be generated, with benefits including time savings, reduced congestion, fewer road casualties, cost savings to BR and bus operations and less expenditure on road schemes.'

Two years later, and after consultancy work had begun into the scope, impact and feasibility of a new light rail system for Croydon, a one day symposium, 'Light Rail for Beginners', was held in the town's famous Fairfield Halls on 26 November 1990. This was organised by Croydon Council, in conjunction with London Transport and the Light Rail Transit Association (LRTA), with the aim of arousing the interest of planners, architects and highway/traffic engineers to the potential of light rail in meeting urban transport needs.

Among a distinguished line-up of speakers from places such as Manchester and the West Midlands, where schemes were already operational, was Scott McIntosh. His chosen subject was 'Vehicles and Infrastructures', and in a 20-minute presentation he shed light on the background to a number of important aspects of Tramlink's subsequent development.

In his talk, entitled 'Vehicles and Infrastructures', McIntosh stressed that, 'it is the total quality of the system which will attract the ridership, particularly the car driver, and it must be borne in mind that any developments in light railway are not simply to capture the existing public transport user.' In the light of the devastating fire at King's Cross underground station (on 18 November 1987), McIntosh also suggested that underground or above ground alignments should be avoided wherever possible:

'…unless there are overwhelming reasons why a tunnel or viaduct is required, the proper place for an intermediate range mass transit system is on the surface and as near as possible to your main established corridors and your central business district and, of course, that means near or in the street.'

Having discussed the essential need for low-floor vehicles and mentioned continental cities such as Grenoble, Geneva and Basel where this had been achieved, McIntosh concluded his talk by noting that global interest in light rapid transit (LRT) schemes had come about through LRT's 'ability to provide a cost-effective, flexible, and user friendly solution to a wide range of intermediate capacity applications', but also sounded a note of caution: 'It must be borne in mind that in the present political climate in the United Kingdom, town planning and environmental objectives are subordinate to a very hard-nosed business approach… We have to convince the Treasury of what we need and, therefore, we must have an approach which produces high quality reliability and predictable cost terms.'

Preparing the ground

Three months after that stakeholder symposium, the first tangible plans for Croydon's future Tramlink system were set out in a report dated 27 February 1991 by Croydon Council's Director of Economic and Strategic Development and the Director of Planning and Transportation. This work was undertaken by a consortium of consultants led by MVA Ltd, Kennedy Henderson, and G. Maunsell & Partners. It noted that, while light rail was reported to be under consideration in many British towns and cities as one means of solving transport problems, only a handful of schemes had received the detailed study and evaluation which had been carried out in Croydon, and that on the basis of this work, the report recommended that, 'a public consultation should now proceed.'

Putting the need for a radical solution to Croydon's transport needs in context, the report noted that Central Croydon 'contains the largest shopping centre and the largest concentration of office floor-space in the South-East outside Central London… Although Croydon is a major business and retail centre, it faces competition from surrounding areas locally, from Docklands, central London, and, in future, King's Cross. The influence of the M25 has made smaller, less congested towns such as Reigate and Redhill increasingly attractive for new offices.

'Croydon's advantages stem from the size and diversity of its economic base. Its extensive workforce, customers from all social strata and a catchment area that extends far beyond the borough's boundaries – especially to the east and

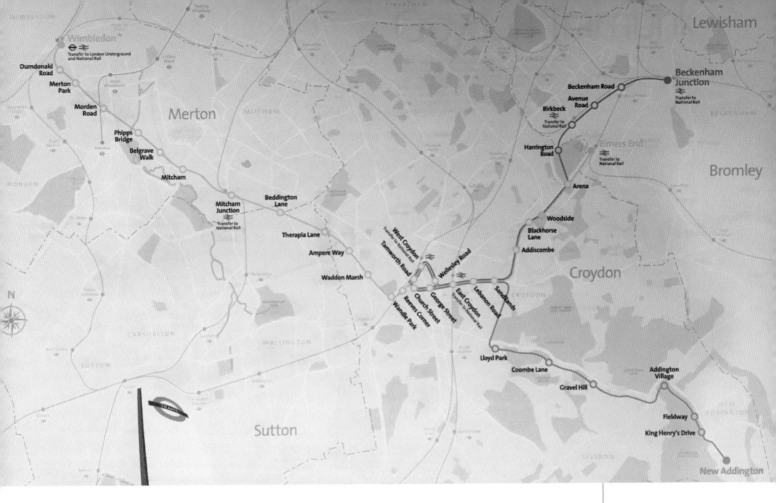

south – provide a magnet for retailing and commercial activity. Effective transport systems are therefore crucial to the maintenance of the Borough's economy, continued prosperity and quality of life.'

Summing up the borough's main transport-related constraints, the report highlighted findings of its 1990 Light Rail study with seven principal conclusions: (i) severe traffic congestion within a three mile radius of central Croydon throughout much of the working day; (ii) a road system which has to carry both Croydon-bound and through traffic; (iii) traffic congestion severely reducing the reliability of bus services; (iv) recruitment of part-time staff increasingly difficult due to unreliable and lengthy journeys; (v) major problems concerning access to car parking; (vi) some major gaps in the bus network causing staff recruitment and retention problems; and (vii) a road system in central Croydon seen as hostile to both pedestrians and car users.

The report warned that if future improvements to the transport system in Croydon were limited to those already committed and anticipated (based on

national and local policies and investment levels) and demand increases in line with real incomes, it can be expected that: '(i) traffic congestion will increase significantly; (ii) bus services will be subject to greater disruption, delay and unreliability; (iii) despite improvements to some rail services, capacity problems will persist at peak times; (iv) conditions for pedestrians and cyclists will deteriorate; and (v) 'rat running' problems will intensify, as more drivers divert to routes through residential areas, with these conditions prevailing for longer periods of the day.'

Making the case for Light Rapid Transit

Forecasts made by computer modelling suggested that, on the basis of continuing with present transport policies, peak-time car movement to central Croydon would increase by between 15 and 20% between 1986 and 2001, while there would be a decline in bus trips of 10 to 15% over the same period. That, however, assumed that

A system map from 2002 shows the three routes (yellow Line 1 from Wimbledon to Elmers End, red Line 2 from West Croydon to Beckenham Junction and green Line 3 from West Croydon to New Addington).

either road capacity could be increased or that motorists would be prepared to put up with much higher levels of congestion. Given the combination of financial constraints and the unpopularity of new road building, these forecasts raised major issues over how to maintain Croydon's economic prosperity, while also preserving its residents' quality of life.

LRT systems will not prevent growth in traffic, noted the Council Report, but do offer an alternative to road building, which will allow more people to make journeys unaffected by congestion. Installing an LRT system could increase the capacity of key routes to and from the town centre, encourage more people to make journeys without cars, and extend accessibility of the town centre to a wider area. In particular, it would be beneficial to bus passengers, who face the prospect of ever increasing disruption to their travel through road congestion, and should help stem the steady decline in bus patronage that had been experienced over many years.

While LRT would not stem the steady growth in road traffic, and its effect on existing levels of congestion would be short-term, the main benefit of such a system would be to insulate those who used it from the effects of other people's travel decisions. It would also protect businesses concerned about reduced accessibility due to increasing road congestion by offering a transport mode that was permanently unaffected by growing congestion, in other words a real choice, without compulsion or restriction.

Why light rail?

After two decades in which interest in new forms of urban public transport had grown steadily around the world, four reasons were put to councillors as the key reasons why a light rail solution should be adopted in Croydon. Firstly, that there was little scope for improving the efficiency of conventional buses by increasing their passenger-carrying capacity or reducing manning levels. Secondly, urban railway had become too expensive to build in all but the most prosperous and densely populated cities. Thirdly, the road networks in major towns and cities, such as Croydon, could no longer cope with peak period travel without unacceptable economic and environmental costs; and, fourthly, energy conservation and environmental pollution had become major social issues.

Looking at the alternative solutions which Croydon might adopt, the report suggested that LRT solutions could bridge the gap between the maximum demand that could be catered for by ordinary bus services and the minimum needed to justify a full-scale railway, putting that at peak levels of demand ranging from 2,000 to 20,000 passengers per hour in each direction. Benefits of LRT over heavy (conventional) rail were sharper curves and steeper gradients, lighter vehicles and small and lighter structures. This all meant faster construction time and lower costs, while the faster acceleration of lighter vehicles meant more stops could be made, so increasing accessibility, ridership and revenues.

Before settling on light rail as the preferred option for Croydon, a number of alternatives were examined, including improved bus services, guided buses (since adopted at nearby Crawley), as well as high-tech options such as Automated Guided Vehicles (AGV). Setting aside guided buses, there were five disadvantages with these alternative solutions, namely that they required total segregation from other traffic, that they were more expensive to construct, were more environmentally intrusive, were less convenient for users and had not been proven on such an extensive and relatively complex network as was required in Croydon.

Guided buses were very much in their infancy in 1991, with only two systems in operation around the world at that time, but it was a solution that warranted further consideration in

Croydon, according to the report. There were, however, a number of important limitations – buses could not be coupled together in peak times, as light rail vehicles could, they would need to revert to street running in the town centre, while in open country and parkland concrete guideways are very intrusive. Given the likely difficulty in attracting private funding to such a relatively unproven technology and the lack of government funding, the report concluded that such a system should be viewed very much as a second best option.

Evaluating existing light rail systems

At the same time as the consultancy consortium was developing its detailed 1991 report into the definition of a light rail system, and assessing its environmental, economic and financial feasibility, Croydon Council independently commissioned a number of other studies into particular aspects of the scheme. Amongst these were the ecological impact of light rail on the Croydon–New Addington corridor and the South Norwood Country Park (though which it would pass); a guide to the Parliamentary Private Bill procedure; and reviews into the most appropriate technology, including a comparison of standard and narrow gauge systems, a review of alternative light rail systems and a comparison between light rail and guided bus systems.

During this study period, members and officers made visits to a number of European cities, to see light rail operation at first hand. Trips included The Hague and Amsterdam, as well as accepting an invitation to see the inauguration of a second tram line in Grenoble. In addition to this – and at their own expense – individual officers visited a host of further towns and cities including Blackpool, Heidelberg, Karlsruhe, Stuttgart, Zurich, Nantes and Lille, with the aim of examining at first hand the operating capacities of different forms of light rail.

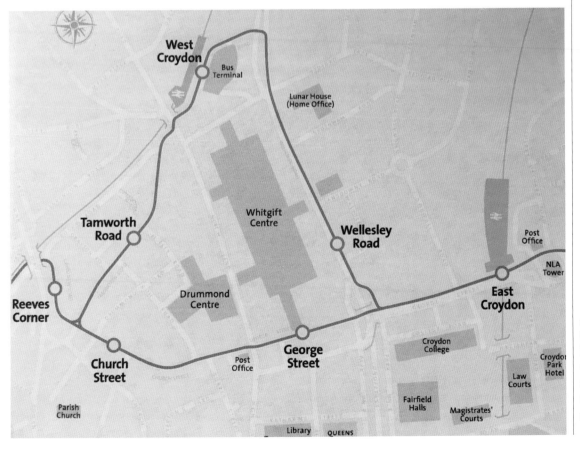

Another 2002 plan, this time of the tram loop around central Croydon, where the as-yet-unopened Centrale stop is shown as Tamworth Road.

In looking at the vast range of options in terms of technology, engineering, systems and routes, there were three principal considerations that formed the basis of the assessment by the Council. Firstly, the system needed to be reliable, provide a significant reduction in journey time, and increase the number of trips into the central area, without any increase in congestion. Secondly, the adverse effects of introducing a new transport system must be capable of mitigation, with any adverse effects on local households and businesses minimised. Thirdly, any new system needed to be capable of attracting private sector interest in its design, construction and operation.

Summing up what was wanted in Croydon, the February 1991 Report considered by the Council's Committees declared that it was, 'to provide a scheme which will be beneficial to Croydon and the neighbouring boroughs, which will prove attractive to both existing public transport users and car users, which will have a strong underlying economic case, and be financially viable and fundable.'

Among key characteristics required of the new system were extensive off-street (segregated) track to provide a fast, efficient and reliable service; few major structures, to avoid unnecessary cost and adherence to accepted design standards to ensure long term operational efficiency and reliability and to avoid high initial costs.

Other essentials were fast journey times to provide benefit to existing public transport users and to reduce congestion by effecting modal shift from car; penetration across the central area to improve accessibility and to assist regeneration of peripheral areas; and a high standard of interchange at the two railway stations (East Croydon and West Croydon) and with bus services throughout the area.

It was in this February 1991 Report that London Transport and the Croydon Council team decided to provisionally adopt the name Tramlink for the new system, which would operate on a mixture of fully segregated track (principally the former railway routes), partially segregated track within the highway and shared carriageway, or street running. In the latter case, any potential for delays would be minimised by reducing other road traffic along the route to a level where congestion would not occur, with priority given to trams at those points where traffic signals controlled road junctions along the new tram routes.

TWO LINES ACQUIRED FROM BRITISH RAIL

Elmers End – Sanderstead

To the eastern side of Croydon, a railway route provided a link from Elmers End, a station on the suburban route from Charing Cross and Cannon Street to Hayes, to Sanderstead, a station south-east of Croydon on the route to Oxted, East Grinstead and Uckfield.

This 6½-mile line had been opened by the London, Brighton and South Coast Railway and the South Eastern Railway in 1885 and enjoyed a twilight existence for most of its 98-year operating life. The double-track route had been electrified in 1935, when intermediate stations at Bingham Road and Coombe Road were rebuilt, and a new half-hourly service introduced, which was far better than anything the line had enjoyed previously.

But traffic never developed in the way it did on other commuter routes across the South-East, and retrenchment soon began. Most weekend services were axed in the 1940s, while a decade later through services to London were replaced outside peak times by a shuttle service to Elmers End.

The last direct services to London were withdrawn in 1976, leaving just a peak-time-only shuttle service until final closure on Friday, 13 May 1983, by which time patronage had fallen below 200 passengers a day and British Rail could not justify necessary improvements to track and signalling along the line.

Services had latterly been operated by two-car 2-EPB 'slam door' electric multiple units, which were more than adequate for the sparse remaining traffic in the line's final years. But the last train was strengthened to six cars on that final Friday, as I vividly remember, having been sent by the News Editor of *The Observer*, where I was working at the time, to cover the closure.

The six coaches of that final departure from Elmers End were packed with enthusiasts, and my photographer for the trip, the famous Jane Bown, who was better known for her royal portraits, was much taken with the experience and got some marvellous shots of the train passing over detonators put on the line by the signalman at Selsdon to mark the sad occasion!

Closure of the Sanderstead route in 1983 did not spell the end of Elmers End as a junction station, as shuttle services continued to operate for another fourteen years along a short branch line to Addiscombe. This left the Sanderstead line just after its first station, Woodside, and continued in a south-westerly direction to a terminus slightly east of central Croydon on Lower Addiscombe Road.

Like the Sanderstead route, it suffered a lengthy period of decline, with loss of direct services to London in the 1970s, closure of its carriage depot, and the loss of its signal box to fire in 1996, when the branch line was reduced to single track. Final closure came in May 1997 and the site was redeveloped for housing, with Addiscombe tram stop later built around 500 metres east of the former station.

Wimbledon – West Croydon

A second railway route that was taken over by Tramlink was another that had enjoyed something of a twilight existence for most of its 142-year life. This was the six-mile-long and predominantly single track route from Wimbledon via Mitcham Junction to West Croydon. It was built by the Wimbledon & Croydon Railway, opening in 1855 and partly built on the track-bed of a much earlier railway known as the Surrey Iron Railway, which ran

A tranquil scene on platform 10 at Wimbledon, where the driver of 2-EPB unit 5664 waits for passengers to join his train to West Croydon.
Photo: Graham Feakins

from Wandsworth to Croydon and became the earliest public railway in the capital when the horse-drawn route had opened in 1803.

The railway was acquired by the London, Brighton & South Coast Railway in 1858 and became part of the Southern Railway at grouping in 1923. Third-rail electrification soon followed in 1930 and, despite sparse passenger traffic, the line enjoyed a significant level of freight traffic between Mitcham Junction and Croydon in particular, where businesses with their own connections onto the line included Waddon Flour Mills, the British Portland Cement Works, Croydon gas works, Croydon power station and, finally, a major power station known as Croydon B, which was opened in 1950.

This once-important freight traffic began to decline by the 1960s and all but ceased in 1973 when Croydon B power station switched from taking rail-borne coal from Betteshanger Colliery in Kent to coal from Durham that was shipped to Kingsnorth in Kent and then delivered by road.

Meantime, passenger traffic remained modest and the two-car electric units which had begun to operate electric services in 1930 were replaced in 1954 by 2-EPB units that remained more than adequate for the irregular passenger service, and were themselves replaced by two-car Class 456 units in October 1991.

Reductions in services had begun in the mid-1960s, with Sunday services withdrawn in June 1965 and the removal of late evening trains from November 1966. The service had enjoyed a basic half-hourly frequency, with additional peak-time services, but these too were withdrawn in May 1971. Services continued for several years after the formal launch of the Tramlink proposals in 1991, but by the time of final closure on 31 May 1997 the line was in a fairly dilapidated state, with graffiti-covered stations and sparse passenger traffic.

Passengers hurry to board unit 456021 with its Wimbledon service in the bay platform (2) at West Croydon station.
Photo: Ian Docwra

CHAPTER 2

PREPARING THE WAY

The initial network – which remains the extent of Tramlink to this day – would connect central Croydon to Wimbledon, Elmers End, Beckenham and New Addington – with trams passing through central Croydon at street level on a one-way circuit that would bring some one million square metres of commercial floor-space within 300 metres of the route, as well as providing a link between East and West Croydon stations.

Under the 1991 proposals, direct services would operate between Beckenham and Wimbledon, with trams from Elmers End and New Addington running only as far as central Croydon, where they would use the one-way circuit to return to their starting point. Journey times would be 16 minutes from New Addington to East Croydon, 15 minutes from Beckenham and 9 minutes from Elmers End, with Wimbledon to West Croydon taking 18 minutes.

In order to improve accessibility to the trams, feeder bus services would be introduced to pick up from nearby residential areas and drop passengers at tram stops. These would be scheduled to match tram arrivals and departures, to minimise waiting times, while in preparation for Croydon's council's Unitary Development Plan, the February 1991 Report said consideration would also be given to the location of 'park and ride' facilities for car drivers – a proposition which was never actually implemented.

Central Croydon

Departing from a major public transport interchange on the bridge outside East Croydon station, trams would travel down the eastern part of George Street, cross the Park Lane/Wellesley Road junction, and continue along the western part of George Street to a stop in the vicinity of North End. To allow the trams to operate, special traffic arrangements would be introduced to remove through traffic from the eastern part of George Street and from the bridge outside East Croydon railway station.

Trams would then proceed at slow speed down Crown Hill and run along Church Street to a stop close to Reeve's Corner. Those bound for Wimbledon would cross the Tamworth Road junction into Cairo New Road and follow the existing road alignment under Roman Way. They would then cross the Sutton–West Croydon railway line on a new flyover, before joining the West Croydon–Wimbledon railway line alongside Wandle Park.

Running in an easterly direction, trams from Wimbledon would follow the same route, before turning into Tamworth Road to join those following the town centre's circular route, proceeding along an existing bus lane before crossing North End and into Station Road to a stop outside West Croydon station and opposite the bus station.

From here they would turn right at the Station Road/Wellesley Road junction and proceed on a segregated track at the centre of Wellesley Road. At a junction with Lansdowne Road new traffic signals would enable trams to cross to the southbound carriageway to serve a stop on the east side of Wellesley Road, before turning left into George Street and returning to East Croydon station.

Croydon to Wimbledon

From Wandle Park, Tramlink's Wimbledon branch would simply follow the line of the railway route, with stops provided at

Wandle Park, Waddon Marsh, Therapia Lane, Beddington Lane, Mitcham Junction, Phipps Bridge Road, Morden Road, Merton Park, Dundonald Road and Wimbledon. By following the existing line, there were few environmental issues to address on this section, but two major pieces of new infrastructure would be a flyover immediately south of Mitcham Junction station, to take Tramlink over the Sutton–London Victoria railway line, and a maintenance depot for the fleet to the north-west of Therapia Lane.

East Croydon to New Addington

What must be the most interesting, and in parts most scenic, of all the Tramlink routes is that to the post-war suburb of New Addington, around five miles south-east of Central Croydon. This comprises a mixture of street running, former railway alignment and tunnels, and finally a long section of running on segregated track through Lloyd Park and Addington Hills, before reaching Addington Village and

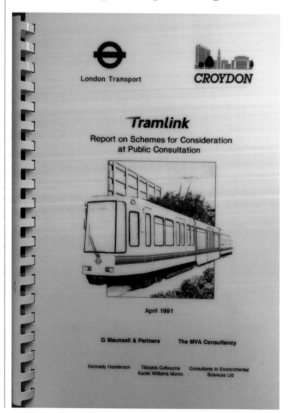

London Transport

CROYDON

Tramlink

Report on Schemes for Consideration at Public Consultation

April 1991

G Maunsell & Partners   The MVA Consultancy

Kennedy Henderson   Tibbalds Colbourne   Consultants in Environmental
                         Karski Williams Monro   Sciences Ltd

A public consultation document on Tramlink, published in April 1991.

then finally a terminus in New Addington at the heart of this major residential area.

Starting at East Croydon, the route would run two-way along Addiscombe Road, as far as a roundabout at the junction of Chepstow Road, with traffic arrangements made to divert other road users away from the route, including improvement work on Chepstow Road, Fairfield Road and Barclay Road. An existing roundabout at the junction with Chepstow Road would be replaced with traffic signals. The route would then cross to the southern side of Addiscombe Road and parallel to the road, with a stop provided (Sandilands) close to the Chepstow Road junction, one of numerous light-controlled junctions where trams would be given priority over other road traffic.

Continuing eastwards, the new line would require the acquisition of front gardens to a number of houses on the south side of Addiscombe Road, along with properties at 90-92a Addiscombe Road, so that the new line could descend onto the disused Elmers End–Sanderstead railway at a point where the New Addington line would diverge from the one heading north towards Elmers End and Beckenham. It was at the 90-degree bend here on the New Addington route that the worst incident in Tramlink's history occurred, the fatal crash on 9 November 2016 which cost the lives of seven passengers (see chapter 9).

Having joined the former railway alignment, the route would continue south in a straight line through three existing tunnels before leaving the former railway at Larcombe Close, the former site of Coombe Road station, where three more residential properties were to be acquired and demolished. The route would then turn east along the southern side of Lloyd Park, on reserved track close to the A212 Coombe Road. Heading eastwards and parallel to Coombe Road, the line would cross Oaks Road then run alongside Coombe Lane – the continuation of Coombe Road – before crossing beneath the main road at the junction of Coombe Lane and Gravel Hill.

The route would then continue along the south side of Gravel Hill, before crossing again to the northern side of this road and into Addington Park, where a tram stop would be located. From here it would cross to the central reservation of a road called Kent Gate Way, before crossing the westbound carriageway to a stop (Addington Village) near the junction of Kent Gate Way and Lodge Lane. The final section of this route would be along the western side of Lodge Lane, where stops would be provided at Fieldway and King Henry's Drive, before taking the central reservation of Parkway and terminating on the western side of Central Parade, adjoining a car park.

Missed opportunities at New Addington

There were a number of aspects of Tramlink's ultimate development in the New Addington area that fell short of what its champion at LT, Scott McIntosh, had originally envisaged, as he recalled in my lengthy interview with him at his present home in Scotland in February 2018:

'In New Addington, of course we had an interchange and feeder buses, which meant that anyone living on the New Addington estate had a much quicker journey – ten minutes on a bus running round an area which never suffers from traffic congestion, then twenty minutes on a tram. We originally sketched out a station which would give you cross-platform interchange between buses and trams, but London Buses scuppered that, because they said the tramway is being built by one contractor, but we want our own contractors building the bus station and therefore the bus station will not be the other side of the platform face from the tram, it will be next to it, in the field next door.

'That was absolutely ridiculous and small-minded, but don't forget that at the time London Buses was not supporting the tramway scheme, even though the LT Board was, they were doing their best to sabotage it and saying we could do it all with buses. Being dragged into providing feeder buses was a difficult enough job, and for all sorts of reasons they continued to want to run a residual service into Croydon. Of course, there was no through ticketing in those days, and even getting them to put the Tramlink logo (the flying T) next to the 'via' point on the bus destination blinds was rejected. It was petty and small-minded.

'We took over a very lightly-used cycle track alongside the main approach road into New Addington, we put a simpler cycle track on the other side of the road, and that is the main segregated approach, where Tramlink is on one side of the road going down into New Addington, then we crossed over and ran in the centre of a grand boulevard (King Henry's Drive), with the route becoming one track and then dividing into two to get round the health centre at the place where buses stand.

A desolate scene at Waddon Marsh, where 2-EPB unit 6264 pauses on its journey to Wimbledon.
Photo: Graham Feakins

'Originally we were going to go another 2-300 metres further on, so that we were right in the shopping area of New Addington. We had quite a good layout at that end, but unfortunately that was disproportionately expensive, which was a pity. What we also wanted to do was something I had seen work very well in Hanover in Germany. Addington Village does not have buses, because the people of Addington Village would not want buses in their nice area, and particularly a bus from New Addington, as the two communities do not get on well together!

'What I had seen in Hanover was a very clever system whereby outside the rush hour you pressed the driver intercom when you got on board the tram, gave the stop you wanted to get off and a name or a code by which you could be identified. Then the tram driver would use the 95% of his dead air-time to call up the local taxi company, so that you would arrive at the tram stop and there would be a taxi waiting for you. TfL might consider such an idea now, because TfL is responsible for taxis, but then we [at LT] did not talk to taxis, so it was another one of those opportunities missed. I think that was a great pity because there is quite an extensive area of upper middle class housing in Addington.'

East Croydon to Elmers End and Beckenham

Diverging from the New Addington route just east of the Sandilands stop, trams bound for Elmers End and Beckenham would take a sharp left-hand turn onto the disused Elmers End–Sanderstead railway line. While the scheme as eventually built saw the elimination of a former railway embankment, the February 1991 proposals were for the route to be built on the original railway embankment, requiring the reinstatement of bridges over Bingham Road and Lower Addiscombe Road, but at a higher level than before to achieve full highway clearance. Five

recently constructed bungalows and part of a sheltered housing development off Teevan Close would need to be acquired and demolished.

From the Croydon Arena, which stands on the west side of the line roughly mid-way between the former Woodside station and Elmers End, trams for Elmers End would continue on the former railway alignment (at that time still used by services to Addiscombe) to terminate in the western platform at Elmers End station. Services to Beckenham would pass east of the Arena on a segregated alignment before joining the existing British Rail line between Crystal Palace and Beckenham junction at a point west of Birkbeck station. This line had been singled some years earlier, so there was space for a single tram line to be built along the south side of this route all the way to a terminus alongside Beckenham Junction station.

Proposed service frequencies and operations

In April 1991 a Report on Tramlink was published jointly by Croydon Council and London Transport. This was based on a public consultation exercise undertaken by the Council, which had shown overwhelming support for the proposed light rail system. In the light of this popular endorsement an evaluation of the original proposals was carried out by the appointed team of consultants, led by G. Maunsell & Partners (Maunsell).

Summing up the rationale for Tramlink, this report noted that the system would, 'facilitate the continued economic development of the Borough and improve the quality of life of those who live, work or use local amenities.' But, it added: 'To be acceptable, a large number of conditions will have to be met. These include a low level of local environmental impact created by, for example, new structures and disruption to traffic flows. In addition, sufficiently robust financial

District Line to Putney,
Fulham & Earl's Court.

SWT to Clapham Junction,
Waterloo & Thameslink
to the City.

Connex/Thameslink
to Balham, Clapham Junction
& Victoria or Tulse Hill,
Peckham & London Bridge.

Connex
to Crystal Palace,
Victoria &
London Bridge.

Connex to Herne Hill,
Brixton & Victoria.

Wimbledon

Dundonald
Road
Merton Park
Morden Road
Phipps Bridge
Belgrave Walk
Mitcham

Connex/Thameslink
to Clapham Junction, Victoria,
London Bridge, Waterloo,
Charing Cross, Bedford & Luton.

Avenue   Beckenham
Road   Road

Birkbeck

Connex to Bromley South
& Orpington.

SWT to Surbiton,
Kingston & the
South West.

Mitcham
Junction

West
Croydon

Wellesley Road

Harrington
Road

Woodside   Arena

Beckenham
Junction

Beddington
Lane
Therapia Lane
Ampere Way
for Ikea and Valley Park
Waddon Marsh
for Purley Way retail parks

Reeves
Corner

East
Croydon

Blackhorse
Lane

Addiscombe

Elmers
End

Connex
to Catford, Lewisham,
London Bridge,
Waterloo & Charing Cross.

Connex/Thameslink
to Hackbridge,
Sutton & Epsom.

Wandle Park

Church   George
Street   Street

Lebanon   Sandilands
Road

Connex
to Eden Park,
West Wickham & Hayes.

Connex/Thameslink
to Purley, Redhill,
Brighton & the
South Coast.

Lloyd Park

Coombe Lane

Addington
Village

Fieldway T31

Headley Drive T32

Connex/SWT to Sutton,
Epsom & Epsom Downs.

Connex/Thameslink
to Gatwick Airport.

Gravel Hill
for Addington Palace

Selsdon Vale T33

Forestdale T31

Fieldway

King Henry's Drive

New Addington

Homestead Way, Vulcan Way T31

Arnhem Drive, Vulcan Way T32

Key

Tramlink Route 1:	Wimbledon - Elmers End
Tramlink Route 2:	Croydon - Beckenham Junction

*During evenings and all Sundays, Route 2 is extended from Croydon to Beddington Lane,
serving also Wandle Park, Waddon Marsh, Ampere Way and Therapia Lane.*

Tramlink Route 3:   Croydon - New Addington

IIIIIIIII Connecting rail services

Connecting bus services

Major bus interchange

Rail interchange

Underground interchange

Airport services

Tramlink ⊖
because trams beat jams

and economic performance is essential to ensure funding.'

On the key issue of service frequencies, it was envisaged that the system would have a peak hour frequency of eight trams an hour (one every 7½ minutes) to and from Wimbledon, Beckenham and New Addington, and four trams per hour to and

from Elmers End. The initial plans assumed that there would be a through service between Beckenham and Wimbledon, while Elmers End and New Addington trams would loop around the central area and return to their point of origin.

Journey speeds, making allowance for passenger stops, reduced speeds on

A plan of the system from its pre-launch publicity leaflet, showing the wide range of rail and bus connections with Tramlink.

street-running sections, and sharp turns, would average between 19 and 24mph for each leg. This would give journey times to East Croydon station of 22 minutes from Wimbledon, 9 minutes from Elmers End, 15 minutes from Beckenham Junction and 17 minutes from New Addington.

To operate such a service the system would need 31 vehicles (including spares) and, although a precise specification had not been agreed at this stage, the planning assumption was for 30-metre long vehicles with a capacity of 220 passengers. These would be electrically-propelled, drawing power from a lightweight overhead wire and be manually driven 'on sight'.

The tram vehicles would have low floors, to allow platforms at about 350mm above rail height, so that it would be possible to arrange level access to at least one door on each vehicle, speeding up boarding times and providing maximum accessibility to those of limited mobility, or those pushing prams.

Traffic management measures would be required to ensure that trams were given priority on street-running sections, with around thirty traffic signals required, together with conversion of existing level crossings on the Wimbledon branch to signal operation. Further measures would be needed in Central Croydon to improve traffic circulation and to protect public transport in general from traffic congestion.

The market for Tramlink

Looking at demand for the proposed new service, the April 1991 Maunsell Report highlighted three distinct categories where journeys would be improved, namely for those people travelling into central Croydon for work or shopping; those travelling to Beckenham and Wimbledon from the local catchment away from Croydon and; movements between the major rail corridors at Wimbledon, West Croydon, East Croydon and Beckenham Junction.

On the basis of computer modelling and actual journey data, the report suggested

that the three hour morning peak period would see about 21,000 passengers boarding Tramlink, with 7,900 on the Beckenham and Elmers End lines, and 6,400 each on the Wimbledon and New Addington lines. More than 7,000 of these passengers were expected to be carried across central Croydon, between East and West Croydon railway stations.

In terms of how these passengers would be won, around 13,000 would be previously bus users, although some bus passengers would continue to use bus to access Tramlink services. Almost all of those people using the then existing British Rail services from Wimbledon to West Croydon and Elmers End to Addiscombe would switch to Tramlink, along with other rail users who were then making circuitous journeys around south London but would switch to the more direct and frequent Tramlink services.

British Rail would gain from some car users attracted to a combination of BR and Tramlink services, given the overall shorter journey times and the improved access which Tramlink would offer to BR services at its four key interchange points (plus Mitcham Junction). Overall, the April 1991 report suggested that 12% of Tramlink's passengers would be former car users – with 2,500 car users switching to Tramlink, and that BR boardings in that peak period would only fall by 800.

Environmental Impact

An assessment of how Tramlink would impact the local environment suggested that the modal shift of car drivers onto the new system would free up road capacity, but be partially offset by the limited impact of trams running on-street and across heavily trafficked highways, such as Gravel Hill and the Chepstow Road junction on Addiscombe Road.

Using scientific methods of traffic and economic evaluation showed that, while the benefit to individual car users would be modest, the cumulative effect would be a benefit of around 1.5 million hours per year, which was valued in monetary terms at £8.37m per year. Looking at the principal junctions between the new Tramlink and existing roads, the consultants' analysis in that April 1991 report suggested there would not be long traffic queues or excessive delays at any of these key points.

Besides its impact on traffic, detailed work was also undertaken into other environmental impacts of the new system, including such matters as visual intrusion, loss of buildings and residential amenity space, and noise/vibration. Investigation was also undertaken into how the environment could be enhanced through integration of Tramlink into built-up urban areas, particularly around key locations such as BR stations.

While the proposed scheme would have adverse environmental impact at specific locations, overall its impact would be very limited. Avoidance of major structures and use of modern lightweight overhead cables would keep its adverse effects to a minimum in built-up areas, with tree planting mitigating its impact in sections passing through open countryside. Being integrated into the built environment meant disturbance was only expected at a limited number of sites.

A number of areas where noise might be an issue were identified, with the installation of double glazing to affected properties suggested as a solution. On the positive side, busy streets where Tramlink was to run would see negligible noise impact and, while noise reduction due to reduced traffic flow would also not be noticeable, fewer buses and cars would mean improved air quality.

Looking at the proposed system on a section-by-section basis, significant effects on the Wimbledon branch would be limited to the planned new bridges over BR routes at Mitcham Junction and at West Croydon. Within central Croydon, care would be needed in George Street/Church Street as they are within a Conservation Area, although listed buildings were not generally affected.

Heading eastwards from central Croydon, there would be a major change to the character of Addiscombe Road and loss of a number of mature trees, as well as a number of residential properties. Care would need to be taken along the former railway corridor from Woodside towards Sanderstead, as this had been designated as a site of Borough Importance for Nature Conservation, but north of Woodside towards Elmers End (still open to BR traffic in 1991) the only change would be an increase in the frequency of services.

On the planned route towards Beckenham Junction there would be impact from Tramlink's development in the South Norwood Country Park, alongside the Arena, as this was a site of Metropolitan Importance for Nature Conservation and would suffer some visual intrusion and noise. Once alongside the BR line from Birkbeck to Beckenham Junction, however, the impact would again be limited to the increased frequency of services.

The major environmental impact of Tramlink would be felt on the Lloyd Park to Gravel Hill section of the New Addington line, which would affect the southern edge of Lloyd Park and Coombe Park, both during the construction phase and subsequent operation. This would

The attractive red livery, which the trams carried until the current green was adopted post-2008, was likened by some to that of Unigate Diaries' milk floats!

lead to the loss of some mature trees and established woodland in Addington Hills which, like South Norwood Country Park, was another site of Metropolitan Importance for Nature Conservation.

Beyond Gravel Hill, and continuing towards New Addington, construction of Tramlink would affect the grounds of Heathfield, a site of Borough Importance for Nature Conservation, with loss of garden area, visual intrusion and noise at Geoffrey Harris House. The remainder of this route would have limited environmental impact, with some noise and perceived severance in the vicinity of the Health Centre at New Addington.

Environmental Impact

As part of the legislative process by which Tramlink eventually got Parliamentary approval, its joint promoters, Croydon Council and London Transport, were required to provide an Environmental Statement, which would identify the potential environmental effects of the project, report on their likely extent and significance, and prescribe measures for their mitigation.

Tramlink's Environmental Statement was prepared by consultants Halcrow Fox and Associates (HFA) and delivered in November 1991, the same month that the Croydon Tramlink Bill was presented to Parliament. This followed extensive public consultation in early 1991, which had led to most of the preferred route being confirmed, with the exception of the Addington Hills section of the New Addington line. Here HFA was asked to consider three alternative and engineering route options, which led to the Council making a slight change to its original proposals and adopting a route which kept close to Coombe Lane throughout and at a maximum gradient of 8%, so keeping as close as possible to existing ground levels.

In their 107-page Environmental Statement, HFA summed up the key environmental impacts of Tramlink under nine headings: land and property; noise and vibration; landscape and visual impact; ecology; traffic; pedestrian safety and convenience; soil and water; heritage; and planning policies. In each case the consultants described the mitigation measures proposed, some of which had already been incorporated in the design and others which were not, but it was being recommended that they should be provided.

Starting with land and property, HFA noted that there would be a loss of twenty residential properties through the development of Tramlink, ten of which were in Addiscombe Road, five in Teevan Close and four in Larcombe Close/Lloyd Park Avenue, along with two commercial properties and strips of open space in a number of parks and alongside Coombe Lane, Gravel Hill, Lodge Lane and Parkway (all on the New Addington line). Proposed mitigation for these losses was the opportunity for replacement housing development on land at Addiscombe Road and modified access arrangements to the remainder of the housing site at Larcombe Close.

Noise and vibration was identified as an issue during the construction phase, particularly in Central and East Croydon, where tracks were being embedded into the streets. Once operational, noise would be a problem on tight corners and at the entrance to the Therapia Lane depot, while vibration could be a problem in Central and East Croydon and on the two flyovers.

Addressing these issues, HFA said construction noise should be screened by hoardings and hours of operation controlled by contract. Noise and vibration from trams should be mitigated by careful design of rolling stock and track, speed limits, and design of the two flyovers to minimise vibration. Noise insulation of affected houses should be considered and noise screening along Lynden Hyrst, in Addiscombe Road, should be provided.

The visual impact of Tramlink – its track, overhead power supply and the trams themselves – would be most noticeable on the sections of new alignment but, in addition to this, properties in Waddon

New Road would have their views obstructed by the Wandle Park flyover and there would be the loss of trees in Addiscombe Road, on the Bingham Road section and along the new alignment to New Addington.

To mitigate these effects, HFA suggested that the construction of Tramlink in Central Croydon provided an opportunity for enhancement of the townscape, with new sympathetically-designed street furniture, paving materials and overhead wires, which should be supported from lighting columns or wall-mounted where appropriate. Outside the central area where tracks run through open space, the ballast should be grassed, with new planting and screening in places where trees were being lost.

A number of interesting ecological issues were identified by HFA, including the loss of land of some ecological interest on the depot site at Therapia Lane and part of a wild flower meadow in South Norwood Country Park. Elsewhere, disturbance to

badger setts could occur on the disused railway between Woodside and Coombe Road and to bats in the tunnels on this section of route.

Proposed measures to deal with these issues were the establishment of what was called an 'ecological buffer' on the edge of the depot site, the fencing off of badger setts during construction and the provision of creeps (underground passages for badgers). Tunnel works should start before summer to prevent bats from establishing a summer roost and bat boxes should be provided.

The impact of Tramlink on both traffic and pedestrians would be largely limited to potential delays and inconvenience during the construction phase and, once operational, to those places where the route crossed roads, particularly in Central and East Croydon. Mitigation measures proposed included a traffic management plan during construction work and signalised crossings once the system was operational, with hazard lights and audible signals on vehicles to warn pedestrians of approaching trams.

Potential issues of soil and water were limited to possible disturbance of contaminated land at Therapia Lane and in South Norwood Country Park during the construction phase, and from the effects of using herbicides for track maintenance on drainage and groundwater during operation. Measures proposed here by HFA were for treatment of any contaminated soil disturbed during the construction phase and for any herbicides used to conform to National Rivers Authority (NRA) standards.

On the heritage impact of Tramlink, HFA noted its potential visual impact on Almshouses in Central Croydon, and at Geoffrey Harris House and lodge in Coombe Road, where vibration could also be an issue. In addition, construction of the two flyovers, the depot and parts of the New Addington line would be in areas of archaeological interest. Sympathetic design of street furniture and sensitive landscaping were proposed, along with measures to reduce the impact of vibration, while the Museum of London was to be kept informed during the construction phase, in the event that there was a need for rescue archaeology along the new route.

Finally, looking at the proposed new system in the light of planning policies, HFA noted that there was an apparent conflict with development plan policies concerning the loss of dwellings and protection of open space. However, their all-important conclusion was that, 'These conflicts are not significant when weighed against policies for improving public transport.'

Financial Performance and Funding

Construction of Tramlink would cost a total of £135m (at 1990 prices), according to the April 1991 report, excluding any financing costs. This figure comprised infrastructure (£76.8m), vehicles (£37.5m), Depot (£10.0m), land and property (£9.7m) and Parliamentary Bill preparation (£1.0m). Included in this estimated total were environmental measures, contingencies, design and management. Annual operating costs (again at 1990 prices) were estimated at £6.18m, of which £4.1m would be the cost of the 200 staff, with the balance made up of energy cost (£0.96m) and maintenance, materials and insurance (£1.12m).

Projected fare revenues were based on estimates of patronage and assumed revenues per passenger kilometre based on average London Transport figures. These implied that 28 million passengers a year would use Tramlink when it was fully established (by 1998, according to the 1991 report) which would generate fare revenues of about £16m a year. This would represent a substantial surplus of fare revenue over operating cost, producing a major contribution to the capital cost of the scheme.

However it was recognised that, in reality, it would take a number of years to build the Tramlink system, and then for its patronage to build up to these projected levels. On the basis that construction could be completed by 1996 and that full revenues would be earned by 1998, a calculation of the Net Present Value (NPV) of the cost and revenue streams over a 30-year period suggested that there would be a funding gap of about £22m (at 1990 prices) between fare revenue and total costs.

At this stage in Tramlink's evolution there had been little exploration of the potential for increasing revenues by such means as premium fares, the sale of advertising space or contributions from property developers who stood to gain financially from its arrival. Nevertheless, the consultants' evaluation recognised that these other potential sources of revenue were unlikely to completely close the funding gap, so that some level of government finance would be required. The justification for this public funding would need to be in the economic benefits delivered by Tramlink.

Economic Benefits

Employing the cost-benefit analysis methodology used to determine the economic performance of transport schemes, the benefits of Tramlink would comprise the time savings through faster journeys by both users of the system and by car drivers faced with reduced levels of congestion. The April 1991 report then looked at the cost and revenue forecasts in the light of the government's assessment framework, by which a scheme is deemed 'worthwhile' for consideration over funding support if revenue plus economic benefits are greater than the cost of the scheme.

In their analysis, the consultants painted a very positive picture of the likely financial performance of Tramlink over a 30-year period, using what were present values and 1990 prices. Over that period the system's capital cost was estimated at £101m and operating costs at £47m, to give total costs of £148m. In addition to the total revenues over this time of £126m, as mentioned above, user benefits were valued at £137m and non-user benefits at £73m, producing total revenue and benefits of £336m, or a surplus over cost of £188m.

The key figure for seeking government funding was the non-user benefits total of £73m, which comprised only two elements, being decongestion (£69m) and a saving to British Rail (then still state-owned) of £4m, with the latter figure reflecting a reduction in rolling stock costs and the saving from no longer operating two loss-making services (Wimbledon–West Croydon and Addiscombe-Elmers End). Comparing this £73m non-user benefits figure to the estimated funding gap of £22m gave a good basis on which Tramlink's promoters could seek some government support. However, with the government indicating that it did not have substantial funds available to support light rail schemes, considerable further work was needed to satisfy government scrutiny.

Taking Tramlink to Parliament

In November 1991, The Croydon Tramlink Bill was deposited in Parliament as a private member's Bill by its sponsor, David Congdon, Conservative MP for Croydon North-East. In its final form, after amendment by committee, the 41-page Bill to allow the project's construction consisted of four sections.

Part I contained preliminary provisions, which included certain provisions of the Tramways Act 1870, the first piece of legislation to clarify and regulate the role of local authorities in promoting tramway development, as well as some of the provisions of the Compulsory Purchase Act 1965 for the compulsory acquisition of land.

Part II of the Bill contained provisions authorising the construction work and all of the consequential road and other alternations, and also included a clause exempting British Rail from the statutory requirement to give closure notice for existing rail services, if that was for the purpose of conversion to Tramlink.

Part III dealt with the acquisition of land and payment of compensation to affected landowners, including granting powers for temporary possession of land where required for construction and its restoration on completion of the works.

Finally Part IV contained a range of miscellaneous provisions, including powers for the promoters to cut and lop trees near the routes when necessary, making it an offence to trespass on Tramlink lines, introduction of a penalty fares regime, and a clause enabling the Transfer of Tramlink to another party by order of the Secretary of State, so paving the way for its handing over to the private sector for design, construction and operation.

An independent review of the proposed scheme

As Parliament scrutinised the private Bill that would pave the way for

Tramlink and lead to a significant degree of financial support from government, Croydon Council sought further validation of the scheme, by commissioning another firm of consultants, GEC Alstom Transportation Projects (GEC), to undertake an independent review of the proposals. Their report, *Croydon Tramlink – Initial Review of the System,* was delivered to the Council, and to Scott McIntosh at London Transport, in April 1992.

In its nine-page assessment of the system's technical and operational features, which was followed by detailed analysis of vehicle performance and route characteristics, GEC draws attention to a number of points where it believes that there is a need for further work. Amongst these, one particular concern (that would in later years be partially rectified) was the number of single track sections in the system as proposed, and the inevitable constraints that would be put on reliability and service frequency.

Looking at each route in turn, GEC began with the Wimbledon branch, by noting that it had five single track sections, due to the restricted width of the existing alignment and the intended single tracking of the two flyovers crossing existing BR lines. 'The number, lengths and separations of the single track sections restrict the operating patterns of the light rail vehicles,' noted the consultants.

Turning to the Beckenham line, their concern here was its 2.8km of single line at the Beckenham end of the route, where it ran parallel to the single line BR route, where service frequency would be determined by the time it took a tram to travel from the easternmost passing loop on this section to the proposed single platform at Beckenham and arrive back at that passing loop.

Other issues regarding the routes highlighted by GEC were the relatively severe gradient of 8% on a section of the New Addington line, which would significantly affect the vehicle design, constraints of the single track loop

around central Croydon, the challenges of operating the system's hub at East Croydon station and the operating sequence of points at the end of the shared section of route east from East Croydon to Sandilands – common to both the Beckenham/Elmers End and New Addington services.

Returning to the constraints of single track sections on the system, GEC reviewed various service frequencies and vehicle capacities, based on peak hour passenger demand forecasts, and an aim to achieve a peak hour capacity in line with those forecast of 1,200 passengers on the Wimbledon branch and 2,400 on both the Beckenham and New Addington lines. After considering a range of different service frequencies, the consultants concluded that the planned infrastructure would restrict the practical operating pattern to either five trains per hour with 240 passengers per vehicle, or six trains per hour with 200 passengers per vehicle.

Commenting in more detail on the infrastructure constraints, GEC noted: 'The fundamental restriction of the use of different operating frequencies and size of vehicle is the long section of predominantly single track at the end of the Beckenham line and the absence of two platforms at Beckenham Junction [another issue that was subsequently addressed]… Crossing of trains [trams] in the double track section between Beckenham and Avenue roads can only be made in a window that is less than one minute wide and, in practice, it may be necessary to stop both trains [trams] whilst the points change. Increased frequency of trains [trams] leads to other delays and significantly reduces the layover time at Beckenham Junction.'

Secondary operational issues attracting comment from GEC were the large number of single track sections on the Wimbledon line and occupancy of platforms at East Croydon for relatively long layovers, which would be enforced by other features of the routes. 'The physical restrictions make it difficult to enhance the passenger capacity of the system in the future,' noted the consultants, who went on to say that it was quite difficult to develop timetables that avoid conflict at the single track sections and/or in Croydon town centre. 'The whole system will be sensitive to the knock-on effects of delays to train [tram] movements,' they warned.

Turning to the design of the tram vehicles, GEC noted that London Regional Transport and Croydon Council's aspirations were for vehicles that were between 2.5 and 2.65m wide, with 2 + 2 seating, 40% of vehicle capacity being seating, low level (350mm) access to one or more doors, and a maximum length of 60m for a pair of coupled vehicles, for minimized effects in Croydon town centre. Besides ruling out high-floor vehicles and 'hump stations' for level access to certain doors – as used on Manchester's Metrolink system – a key design issue was the severe gradients of the New Addington line, which would require the vehicle to have all axles motored, so that an operational vehicle would be able to push a partially defective vehicle up the steepest 8.4% grade on this line, if necessary.

The consultants considered a wide variety of vehicle types, amongst which were Siemens-designed vehicles for the new super-tram network in Sheffield and a GEC Alstom design for Nantes in France, both of which were only partially low-floored and both of which were longer than the 30m aspiration in Croydon. Having looked at vehicles of various lengths and passenger capacities, GEC concluded that attaining a seated capacity of 40% would be difficult and that only a 200-passenger capacity vehicle met the twin objectives of a coupled pair of vehicles being not more than 60m in length and practical operation on the route network as planned.

2-EPB unit 5752 approaches Woodside Junction in April 1971 with a service from Addiscombe to Elmers End, with the rusty lines of the route to Sanderstead diverging to the left.
Photo: Graham Feakins

CHAPTER 3

WINNING PARLIAMENTARY APPROVAL

From the start of Tramlink's development it was always anticipated that the ultimate developer/operator would be a joint public/private sector undertaking, with London Transport and Croydon Council taking responsibility for land acquisition, gaining Parliamentary approval and granting highway authority for the system. Design, construction, operation and maintenance would then be the responsibility of the winning private sector bidder, which would most likely be a consortium, in view of the variety of disciplines required.

Scott McIntosh has a somewhat jaundiced recollection of his dealings with Government in the early days of Tramlink's gestation: 'The Treasury decided that they had their PFI team and they were going to show us how to do things brilliantly – these notable people who brought us the crash of 2008 were going to tell us how to do a technical job. I did complain, but David Bayliss looked at me and said "our hands are tied". The Chief Secretary to the Treasury at the time was Michael Portillo. I had been at university with Michael, so I wrote him a few letters, getting progressively more insistent that this was somewhat silly and I kept on getting letters back from his minions saying "Government policy is…"'

'The best move I made was when I struck up a really good relationship with Steve Norris, the junior Minister of Transport, who said to me that if ever I wanted to have a chat, come round first thing in the morning. We have 'morning prayers' at 08.30 in the morning he explained, which is when the ministerial team sits down with the civil servants to discuss what issues have occurred overnight.

'He said if you come before morning prayers we can have a chat, so I used to go and see him and I remember on one occasion saying, look this isn't going to work the way you think it is, and he looked at me and smiled and said "government policy is blah blah blah… the private sector knows best… everything will be perfect." At which point his 'Bernard' poked his head around the door and said "morning prayers, Minister". Norris said "you'll have to excuse me," and as he got to the door, turned back and said, "and Government policy is complete bollocks" and walked out!'

Given the government's requirement for close involvement of the private sector in delivering Tramlink, to the extent that it was also to be involved in the development process, the promoters established a Project Development Group (PDG), following a competitive process, in October 1992. Joining Croydon Council and London Regional Transport were three private sector partners – Tarmac, AEG and Transdev – to collectively provide the necessary experience in construction and project management, railway engineering and light rail operations.

'The PDG partners were individually selected on the basis that their presentations convinced us they knew what they were doing and would deliver,' explains McIntosh. 'That was a little bit of a concession we managed to screw out of Michael Portillo, because we said we did not want to be lumped with a pre-formed consortium, as had been the case with the DLR one [GEC and Mowlem].

CROYDON TRAMLINK [H.L.]

(AS AMENDED IN COMMITTEE)

EXPLANATORY MEMORANDUM

This Bill enables London Regional Transport ("the Corporation") and the Croydon London Borough Council ("the Council") to develop and operate a system of light rail transit ("Tramlink") connecting the centre of Croydon to Wimbledon, Beckenham and New Addington.

The Wimbledon and Beckenham branches of Tramlink will make use of existing or former British Rail railway routes while much of the New Addington branch will consist of new railway lines. The central section in Croydon will consist of tramways connecting East Croydon and West Croydon British Rail stations. The Bill empowers the Secretary of State to make a transfer order transferring the necessary functions under the Bill to enable a private sector operator to construct and operate Tramlink.

PART I

PRELIMINARY

Part I of the Bill contains preliminary provisions.

Clause 3 incorporates, subject to modifications, general enactments relating to railways contained in the Railways Clauses Consolidation Act 1845 and the Railways Clauses Act 1863, and disapplies certain other railway enactments.

Clause 4 incorporates, with modifications, certain provisions of the Tramways Act 1870.

Clause 5 applies, with modifications, the provisions of Part I of the Compulsory Purchase Act 1965 to compulsory acquisition of land under the Bill.

PART II

WORKS

Part II contains provisions authorising the construction of works.

Clause 6 authorises the making and maintenance by the Corporation of the works specified in Part I of *Schedule 1*, which include the new tramways and other new railways comprised in Tramlink. The lines and situations of those works are shown on the deposited plans.

1

These were DBFO [Design, Build, Finance and Operate] contracts, and I well remember the Finance Director of Mowlem saying at some formal dinner we were all attending that "as far as I am concerned it stands for Design, Build and F*** Off".'

Choice of PDG Partners

Scott McIntosh has a vivid recollection of how the three PDG partners were chosen: 'As equipment manufacturer we ended up with what was then called Adtranz

London Transport
Croydon Tramlink

Information Memorandum

CROYDON

The formal document issued to prospective tenderers, published by LT and Croydon Council in June 1995.

[AEG], which had just completed its first 100% low-floor tram – it is one which went to Bremen and later to Berlin. It was not perfect, but had a lot of really good points about it; it had body-mounted motors and very simple bogies. I remember being in the car sheds at Bremen and I asked a German engineer about changing the bogies and he told me that they could generally get them out in 45 minutes. I said "45 minutes!" and he replied "I know, once we are more practiced we will have it down to half an hour!"

'The ride quality was a bit of an issue – I was a bit worried for Croydon because, with bogies at the centre of each vehicle,

at high speed the tram develops a slight rolling action and I thought that we had a lot of 80km/h sections on the Croydon system, but their people were really good. It was at a time when they were the innovative ones – Siemens were just offering us some lumpy old lard bucket and the Italians were hard to take seriously and you had to be careful that they had not left you a brown envelope stuffed with fivers!

'We then found a contractor [Tarmac]. Contractors are pretty difficult to choose one against another, because they may turn up and say that they have built this or that, but they are simply management companies, and they hire in whatever contractors they can get their hands on.

'Finally we chose as the operator Centrewest London Buses [Transdev]. There were two reasons for that. The lesser reason was that it was one of the management buy-outs from London Buses, and this was a time when the newly-privatised bus companies didn't bid for areas of London to run, they could bid route-by-route.

'Secondly, given that Centrewest was a very ambitious company, it was quite likely that it would bid for the feeder routes that would connect with Tramlink and then we could end up with an integrated system, which is something everyone else seems to be able to manage, but we can't. But the major reason was that Centrewest was part-owned by [Sir] Peter Hendy – he had led the management buy-out team and was the largest shareholder in the company. Hendy was very enthusiastic and later became Transport Commissioner – he knows a lot about transport and is also a closet tram enthusiast!

'Having chosen the three firms, we then put them in a room and said "don't come out of this room until you have agreed to work together." If at the end of two days you emerge and say you cannot work together, then fine and it's all off. None of you have the job and we hold the beauty contest all over again. You can come back

A view looking towards Sandilands Junction from Woodbury Close, showing trackwork nearing completion on 23 May 1999. (Photo: Stephen Parascandalo)

into the contest, but it is as if nothing had happed before that."

'What you have to come out with is an agreement that you will work with us to develop the performance specification. When we have agreed that performance specification you will go ahead and build it, you will provide parent company guarantees as to the funding being made available and you will bear any cost over-runs or losses, because it was to be a design, build, finance and operate contract.'

The PDG process meant that there was private sector involvement at an early stage in the project's development, before any details were actually finalised. It meant that a number of key parameters could be determined by a potential concessionaire (once disbanded, the three PDG partners would subsequently be one of the short-listed parties to develop and operate Tramlink), who would need to be satisfied that any finalised scheme was capable of attracting private sector funding.

As interested parties in the subsequent bidding process (which they did not win) the three PDG partners were seen as a proxy for the ultimate concessionaire during the project's development phase, offering a 'bankable' view from the private

sector of the actual grant requirement that would need to be financed by central government. The whole project development process at Tramlink was regarded as an innovative approach to the problems of reconciling public sector interests in infrastructure with the realities of private sector funding and operation, with lessons learned from the Tramlink PDG providing valuable experience for future public/private sector cooperation.

While selection of a construction company (Tarmac) and an operator (Transdev) were logical choices, the inclusion of an equipment supplier (AEG) was a less obvious inclusion in the group. Given that its role was not immediately clear, Scott McIntosh from London Regional Transport invited a Dutch engineer named Nico Dekker, then working for Acer Consultants Ltd, to begin what went on to become a long term association with Tramlink, by becoming Technical Liaison Manager for AEG on the project, effectively managing the firm into the PDG consortium.

Over the next two years (1992-4), the PDG worked to develop detailed specifications for the system as well as reviewing its economics, balancing forecast revenues against anticipated operating costs and, crucially, preparing a formal submission to the Department of Transport for financial support under Section 56 of the 1968 Transport Act (detailed below). The PDG also helped to draw up the commercial terms on which the project would be undertaken, and a draft Concession Agreement for discussion with the Department of Transport and the Treasury.

Consulting the public

At the time McIntosh began work on the project, there was a well-established LT principle that you didn't do too much, because if you told the public anything it just gave them opportunities to throw things back at you later, so the aim was to

Overhead lines being installed at New Addington on 10 August 1999.
(Photo Stephen Parascandalo)

in those days – it was just the Croydon light rail proposal – and I must not refer to anything as trams, because we did away with those in 1952 and we weren't going there again!

'The meeting got very hostile, and Dennis said to me at one point "I think you're on your own with this lot, I'm going for a fag," and just sidled off the stage! So I thought that the best thing to do was show the pictures, so I gave them the first fifty slides and this little old lady stood up and said, "When I heard that you were going to build a railway, I thought it was going to be like the underground down my road, but I've had a look at your pictures and what you are talking about is trams!" I thought, Oh f*** it, and said "yes dear, it is trams," and she replied, "Oh, that's alright then, they was wonderful in the blitz!"

'We tried to work with people, but there were some we simply couldn't, such as one I called the squirrel woman and others by the Wandle Park flyover, where quite obviously somebody had got them wound up, and I suspect that somebody had told them all that if they screamed loudly enough then LT would offer to buy all your houses and you will be shot of them.

'My biggest meeting was the Fairfield Halls one, and my smallest was the Purley Women's Gas Users Lunch, where I think I addressed six people! I had a young graduate, who later went on into public relations, and this was his first proper job. He was my PR man and he went to a lot of small meetings and we answered every single letter we received, except for one man, who wrote every single week and eventually Croydon Council got legal opinion to say that this man was just being vexatious, so I wrote to him telling him that he was being vexatious and that we were not going to write to him again.

'I was not afraid of doing public meetings and Dennis [Coombes] was quite good at it, though he wouldn't do it as much as I did. We just talked and talked and talked and we did things like hold conference calls – dial-in phones had just been developed – and we published the

do the minimum. McIntosh took a rather different approach, and firmly believed in telling people as much as possible, while being honest and up-beat about the project, a strategy that would also help flush out the quality of any opposition.

'In Croydon I was very determined from the beginning that I would talk to anybody at any length and at any time about the project,' he recalls. 'We started with a few of the very traditional public meetings and I particularly remember one in the Fairfield Halls – that is a big place and we must have had about 600 people – they were the ones from Addiscombe Road and the Whitgift Estate who were all worried about property values.

'Dennis [Coombes] was on the platform, David Bayliss's deputy, and me, and I was going to do a presentation. This was in the days before PowerPoint, when I had a projector and several hundred colour slides, showing examples of how trams were done in other places. The audience was pretty hostile, and one of the things I had been instructed was that I was not, *under any circumstances*, to refer to anything as a tram! The DLR had light rail vehicles and this would be a light rail system. We hadn't got a name for it

results. I was accused at one meeting of doctoring the photographs to hide all the horrible wires that were going to be all over the place, and I did say to them that if I could do that I would be working in the film studios at Elstree, rather than sitting in a parish hall at 8.00pm being insulted! I think it worked, because it was the first time that a lot of people had ever known LT to come out – not be dragged out kicking and screaming.'

Picking a name

Picking a name for the planned new system was a key milestone, so McIntosh convened a meeting with all those at Croydon Council involved in the project, along with a few others, including a representative of the *Croydon Advertiser* and told them that they needed to choose a name for the system. McIntosh favoured reviving the old name for the tramways in Croydon, which was South Met. In Croydon there had been two tramway systems, one owned by Croydon Corporation and one by the London & Suburban Traction Company, which had the longest name in the business – the South Metropolitan Electric Lighting & Tramways Company.

'I thought South Met was quite a nice name, but for some reason the Council didn't like it, so we went through all sorts of possible names including the *Croydon Shopper* and the *Croydon Hopper'*, recalls McIntosh. 'Following on from BART [Bay Area Rapid Transit] in San Francisco I also quite liked *Croydon Advanced Passenger Transport*, but eventually someone from Croydon Council came up with *Tramlink*, because *Thameslink* had just been launched. I said: "That solves it, can you write to me and suggest that name, because my bosses will go ballistic when they find out!" That was it, and the scheme became Tramlink after that and we all referred to it that way and people all recognised it as being something less threatening and frightening.

'What was interesting was that we went out and did our first telephone canvases and the *Croydon Advertiser* did a canvas very early on, and we had something like 55% of respondents in favour from day one. We had the people who didn't want to lose their homes, there were the driving maniacs who didn't want to see any road capacity reduced, and there was the 'it'll never happen' brigade, but there was not much serious opposition from people who didn't have a vested interest in stopping it going ahead. The attitude from a lot of people was that the roads in Croydon are so full of cars already, so anything that will reduce traffic is welcome.'

One notable change to the system's identity took place in October 2008, shortly after its takeover by TfL (as described below), when it was announced that it would in future be known as Tramlink, rather than Croydon Tramlink. The aim of this change was to reflect the inter-urban nature of the network, which might have Croydon at its hub, but was serving places some distance away and in future could be further extended.

Parliament debates Tramlink

At the same time as the PDG was finalising outline details of the system and paving the way for government financial support, the *Croydon Tramlink Bill* was being steered along its lengthy passage through Parliament. It had been deposited in November 1991 as a private member's procedure by David Congdon, Conservative MP for Croydon North East. Having passed through the House of Lords and committee stage with no hold-ups, the key debate in the House of Commons came with its second reading at 7 pm on 21 July 1993 – a year to the day before what became the *Croydon Tramlink Act* was granted Royal Assent on 21 July 1994.

While the eventual vote on the Bill, after a debate lasting almost three hours, was overwhelmingly in favour (Ayes 199: Noes 8), it did allow those opposed to Tramlink, or having issues with aspects of the scheme, an opportunity

Another view of 2535 on the first ever powered test run through Croydon on 16 June 1999, seen here in Crown Hill. (Photo: Stephen Parascandalo)

to air their concerns. Most prominent of these dissenters was Piers Merchant, Conservative MP for Beckenham, who was vehemently opposed to the scheme, despite what now seem obvious benefits to his constituents.

Another to speak out, and later vote against the Bill, was Andrew Bennett, Labour MP for Denton and Reddish in Greater Manchester, who responded to Congdon's opening remarks by asking him why the promoters had not responded to petitions from the Open Spaces Society and the Ramblers Association, suggesting that compensatory open space be provided for the public open space required by Tramlink.

Congdon declared that the promoters believed that the impact on open space would be limited and that they were therefore not able to meet his demands, adding that it was significant that the Bill enjoyed the support of the Association of Croydon Conservation Societies. He was then challenged by the Beckenham MP, who suggested that the solution to congestion problems would be to make better use of existing British Rail infrastructure, and questioned how running trams down the centre of roads in Croydon would ease traffic congestion.

Congdon's answer to this was that quite a lot of BR line was being used, but that it was quite inflexible and difficult to extend to other areas. On the issue of congestion, he declared, 'it is possible, with good design and traffic management measures, to minimise any impact that may be created to enable the light rail to run on existing road.'

Wimbledon and Beckenham

Two issues that would later be addressed in the final design of the scheme were the locations of terminus stations in Wimbledon and Beckenham. The first of these was raised by the MP for Wimbledon, Charles Goodson-Wickes, who followed Merchant's logic over the using of existing BR lines by suggesting that it was 'nonsensical' for the Wimbledon terminus not to be at the existing Wimbledon station (the terminus was originally proposed to be south of the road overbridge at Wimbledon station).

Here Congdon had good news, as British Rail had indicated a willingness to review its earlier refusal to allow Tramlink to use platform 10 in the station: 'A feasibility study by BR has

Police motorcyclists accompany 2535 as it heads along George Street towards East Croydon station with the inaugural powered test run on 16 June 1999. (Photo: Stephen Parascandalo)

stated that in principle it is prepared to allow Tramlink to use platform 10', he asserted, 'I know that the promoters hope that discussions with BR will continue…as the scheme would greatly benefit from a full interchange at Wimbledon station.'

Turning to the location of the Beckenham terminus, Merchant asked for confirmation that the interchange at Beckenham Junction would not actually be in the station itself, but one like that proposed at Wimbledon, which would involve passengers connecting between BR and Tramlink services coming out of one station, walking down the road and going into another. He added that there was strong bipartisan opposition to Tramlink in Beckenham, from both the local Labour and Conservative parties. Congdon's response was to claim that the planned interchange 'was a reasonable way of enabling people to transfer from one service to another'.

After Merchant had expressed concern at Tramlink crossing South Norwood Country Park, within his constituency, Congdon stressed how much effort was being made to be environmentally sensitive in development of the system. Taking the New Addington branch as an example, he said that earlier proposals for the route to run straight across Addington Hills – an attractive wooded area – had been replaced by the working party developing the project in favour of a route which ran along the edge of the road and not straight through Addington hills: 'This is a very good example of the promoters' desire not to cause environmental difficulties, particularly to valuable open space,' he asserted, 'I am pleased to say that that sensitive approach to crucial environmental issues adopted by the working party and the promoters has underpinned the development of the scheme.'

A further question for the Bill's promoter came from Bennett, who sought confirmation that, if granted the Royal Assent, the whole scheme would be completed as one entity 'or is there a risk that the private sector may decide that one bit is financially viable and the other bits are not?'

Congdon responded by saying that, as he understood it, 'all parts of the scheme will be built and financed by the private sector and that it will stand or fall in its entirety… The key part of the scheme is that the commercial risks and responsibilities rest with the private sector. It will provide the major part of the funding. An element of Government funding could well be required, but that would have to reflect the public benefits that the scheme would generate, especially to other route users.'

Backing for Tramlink

The Bill's promoter then went on to talk about the scale of backing for Tramlink: 'The scheme enjoys the unanimous support of Croydon Council, which has voted in favour of it, and is strongly supported by the Croydon Chamber of Commerce and Industry, which is a consortium of 1,300 local businesses. The scheme is also supported in principle by local trade associations, environmental groups and the neighbouring boroughs of Bromley, Sutton and Merton. A high degree of public support for it was expressed during the consultation period… Tramlink provides an exciting opportunity to introduce a modern, clean, reliable and, above all, safe transport system, which will enhance the quality of public transport in a large area of south London.'

After Bennett and Merchant had both returned to the theme of lost open space, Congdon pointed out that South Norwood Country Park had only been created a few years earlier, that Tramlink would take nowhere near the 13 acres of it that protesters had suggested, and the fact that its 150 acres had been designated open space, rather than given over to housing and light industry, as previously intended,

showed the seriousness of the council in creating open space.

Two local MPs then joined the debate, with Richard Ottaway (Conservative, Croydon South) expressing support for the Bill, but noting that the scheme did not affect the south of the borough and lamenting the lack of new road building in south London. He then proceeded to list four concerns about the scheme – raising doubts about its funding, worries over the disruption which its construction would cause, questioning what he termed 'the British content of the proposed scheme' (only one of the three PDG members being British) and finally expressing the hope that a spur might be built to Purley, where he had found 'overwhelming local enthusiasm' for such an idea.

Fellow local MP Sir Paul Beresford (Conservative, Croydon Central) raised concerns over the impact on residential properties, singling out Lynden Hyrst whose residents, 'feel that when they step onto the pavement the Tramlink will virtually run across their toenails.'

Setting out the government's position on Tramlink, Steve Norris, the Minister for Transport in London, noted that this was essentially a private-sector project, in accordance with the government's policy of involving private sector skills and capital to the maximum extent possible, to provide the best value for money for both taxpayers and users of the system. Norris went on to talk about the PDG, pointing out that the three private companies were funding the development work themselves, and that they were working to prepare a development brief, which would then be put out to tender within European Commission (EC) rules.

If the PDG team did not ultimately win the contract, the costs they have borne so far would be passed on to the successful bidders. On the question of government funding, Norris stated, 'The Government will consider any application for grant on its merits by examining the public benefits that will be secured by the scheme – the non-user benefits – and relating them to the amount of grant sought.'

Cross-party support in Croydon

One final local MP to join the debate and express support for Tramlink was Malcolm Wicks (Labour, Croydon North-West), who backed the scheme for three major reasons, social, economic and environmental. On the social point, he said that one third of the 25,000 residents of New Addington did not have access to a car, a peak-time bus journey to the centre of Croydon could take 45 minutes, and unemployment among men in New Addington was 18.8%.

It would bring economic benefits, as was recognised by many business people in Croydon, while its environmental benefit would be in enabling people to opt for public transport rather than take a car. Challenged on this final point by the MP for Beckenham, who said the promoters only expected 10% of Tramlink users to be switching from cars, Wicks pointed out: 'As in many other towns and cities, atmospheric pollution in Croydon is above EC guidelines and we should be concerned about that. I would welcome a 10% impact.'

As the near three-hour debate drew to a close, the MP for Beckenham (Piers Merchant) continued to attack all aspects of the Bill ('I do not like it at all') and raised a number of alternative suggestions to the proposed route to Beckenham. He suggested that the line be terminated at Elmers End, where there was enough land to build a park-and-ride facility (something which the promoters were keen to avoid anywhere on the system), but if it was felt that the line should be taken closer to Beckenham, then why not run it alongside the existing British Rail Hayes line, where Clock House station was as close to the centre of Beckenham as was Beckenham Junction?

After raising the possibility of enhancing existing (indirect) BR services between Beckenham and Croydon, Merchant went on to rubbish the promoters' passenger forecasts for Tramlink: 'I have examined in extreme detail the assessments of

A second view of 2536 followed by 2533 as they approach Blackhorse Lane with the first powered run to Beckenham on 7 October 1999.

(Photo: John Bradshaw)

the predicted number of passengers who would travel on every section of tramway… I believe that the promoters' figures for the use of the Tramlink system are deeply and fatally flawed. I simply do not believe that the custom exists to make the system a viable project.' History was to prove otherwise!

Seeking financial support from Government

Having secured a substantial majority for the Croydon Tramlink Bill's second reading, one of the key tasks now facing the promoters was to secure government funding for part of the capital cost, under what was known as Section 56 of the 1968 Transport Act. After a number of different service patterns had been examined, this submission by the PDG adopted what it called a 'base case' level of service, comprising peak hour frequencies of six trams an hour between Wimbledon and Beckenham, eight trams per hour to

New Addington and four trams per hour between Elmers End and East Croydon.

Journey speeds, including stops, street running and sharp turns, would average between 19 and 24mph, giving journey times to East Croydon station of 25 minutes from Wimbledon, 20 minutes from Beckenham Junction and 20 minutes from New Addington, times that were somewhat slower than those in the April 1991 study by Maunsell.

As discussed above, there was a compelling rationale for the development of Tramlink, in an area where its considerable economic success had put serious strain on the local road network. In particular, the PDG's submission noted that severe traffic congestion was occurring within a three mile radius of central Croydon throughout the day; unreliable bus services meant late arrival of staff at work was commonplace; recruitment of part-time staff was becoming more difficult because of extended journey times; availability of and access to car parking was a major

2530 operated the first powered run to New Addington on 1 September 1999 and is seen here at King Henry's Drive. (Photo: Stephen Parascandalo)

The first tram to arrive under power at New Addington was 2530 on 1 September 1999. (Photo: Stephen Parascandalo)

problem; and the road system in Croydon was perceived as being hostile to both pedestrians and car users.

Set against this backdrop, the PDG made a strong case for the new system: 'Tramlink is by far the most important current initiative, representing a major improvement in the quality of public transport provision, and providing a much enhanced orbital link across the area. With virtually complete segregation from the effects of traffic congestion, Tramlink also represents a major investment in a future public transport system which will not deteriorate as traffic conditions worsen.'

Peak periods would see about 1,800 Tramlink passengers transfer from car, around 11,000 would transfer from buses, with 5,500 transferring from the existing rail services, with a further 3,300 peak hour trips resulting from the generation of additional passengers through the enhanced frequency provided by Tramlink and by penetration of the central area of Croydon and the linking of East and West Croydon stations.

By the time of the Section 56 submission in 1994, the expected costs of building Tramlink had increased to around £154m (at 1993 prices), although phasing of construction reduced this figure to about £124m. With estimated operating costs of £55m a year and revenues of £144m, that produced an anticipated operating surplus of £89m and meant that what was called the net 'public sector financial gap' was about £35m. User benefits from

Tramlink were valued at £194m, primarily representing the value of travel-time savings by those transferring to the new system from car, bus or BR services, while non-user benefits – principally travel time saved by remaining road users, were valued at £123m.

On the basis of the cost-benefit analysis used to assess other London rail schemes, Tramlink's estimated benefit:cost ratio was 2.53:1. The criteria for awarding Section 56 grants required that non-user benefits alone should exceed the required public sector funding, so not only did the system have a very positive case in terms of benefit:cost, but its £123m of non-user benefits was far in excess of the £35m public sector financial gap. All these forecasts were made on the basis of no change in the status quo in terms of existing public transport, and took no account of the potentially major impact of bus deregulation, as discussed in detail below.

No deregulation of buses in Croydon

One change in the legislative environment that would work in favour of Tramlink concerned deregulation of buses. The Conservative Government had deregulated buses outside London in 1986, and had been set to do the same in London. But in November 1993 the government decided not to implement deregulation in the capital, and instead to press ahead with privatisation of LT's individual bus businesses. For LT, it was vitally important that Tramlink be seen as part of an integrated transport network and be included in its travelcard and concessionary fares systems, a point acknowledged by Steve Norris, Minister for Transport in London, during debate of the Tramlink Bill in the House of Commons.

An estimate of how deregulation would have seriously damaged Tramlink's prospects can be seen in the Section 56 submission for government funding by the PDG. While most of that submission assumed that local bus services would

A test to ensure there is adequate clearance between trams and buses at the Lebanon Road stop. (Photo: Stephen Parascandalo)

2561 passes Lebanon Road bus stop on 6 November 2018 with a Wimbledon service.

A throng of passengers wait to board 2546 at Church Street on 31 October 2018, one of the few sections of the present system served by trams in the past.

remain regulated throughout the life of the project, it noted that bus deregulation in London remained government policy.

On the assumption that it would take the same form as deregulation of buses outside London had taken in 1986, a section of the submission document considered the financial consequences of deregulation on Tramlink, assuming that it would lead to pressure on multi-mode tickets such as the travelcard, increased competition and potentially lower fares from bus operators and lower bus operating costs through changes to working practices or lower real wages, some of which might be adopted by Tramlink.

Even without deregulation, Tramlink would face a degree of competition from buses, as there would always be some routes which served passenger journeys that could also be made by Tramlink. However it was likely that services in direct competition with the new system would be cut short, withdrawn – as was the case with the X30 West Croydon–New Addington service – or used as feeder

services, because Tramlink would provide a faster and more reliable service. In a deregulated market, however, experience elsewhere showed that bus operators were willing to persist with uneconomic levels of competition for a variety of perceived strategic market share benefits.

In a table that modelled a range of different potential scenarios, the Section 56 submission document showed that the anticipated £35m funding gap for the Tramlink system could significantly increase. In a worst case scenario, with bus speeds increased by 20% from their current level, Tramlink patronage would fall by between 26 and 29% from its forecast level and the financial gap would more than double to £73m. What the analysis showed clearly was that relative speed, rather than frequency of competing bus services, was the most important factor in Tramlink's financial performance – a 20% increase in bus frequencies would only reduce Tramlink patronage by 3%, while the 'competitive' bus network only reduced its patronage by between 6% and 10%.

CHAPTER 4

BUILDING AND OPENING TRAMLINK

A significant amount of development work was carried out by the PDG between 1992 and 1994 to refine the scheme, with specifications set out that would leave scope for initiative by the expected range of bidding consortia in respect of funding, development, operations and maintenance. These specifications were set out in a document prepared by the PDG dated 10 February 1994 and entitled 'Croydon Tramlink – System Description Base Scheme', which detailed every aspect of the proposed system from patronage to power supply, and civil works to control and communications.

In terms of anticipated patronage, the PDG document said that the system would be based on an estimated patronage for the 7-10 am weekday peak of 21,025, with the system designed to handle 44% of that total during the busiest one hour of the peak period. The track layout was revised from earlier work in 1992 to include extensive single track sections, but the PDG team noted that certain operationally critical sections are currently being investigated, and warned that, 'it is believed that the infrastructure savings resulting from extensive single tracking may not be operationally efficient and may even necessitate additional vehicles.'

Track layout diagrams in the document, provided by PDG partner Tarmac, showed a long stretch of single line from Merton Park to just north of Therapia Lane on the Wimbledon branch, single track on the branch from Arena to Elmers End and lengthy sections of single line on the Beckenham route where it ran parallel

to the operational British Rail single line, with just two short sections of double line and two platforms at the Beckenham Junction terminus. The only route to be double track throughout – with the

A pre-launch publicity leaflet heralding the arrival of Tramlink.

BUILDING AND OPENING TRAMLINK • 55

exception of its terminus approach – would be the New Addington line.

Given its role as one of the PDG partners, the base scheme document assumed the use of an existing AEG-manufactured vehicle, known as the GT6N, which was already in service in Bremen, Munich and Augsburg and on order in several other cities. This was a standard 2.3 metre wide three-section vehicle with a passenger capacity of 185, which increased to 211 if a wider 2.65 metre variant was used, and was the preferred choice of the operating partner within the PDG (Transdev) on the basis that it offered greater flexibility than a four-section car. Based on a revision of anticipated service patterns, the PDG said that the system would need 24 of the 2.3m wide vehicles or 22 if the wider 2.65m option was selected.

Planning for future expansion

One important requirement was to allow for the Tramlink system to be expanded in the future by 25%, meaning a 25% increase in the number of passengers carried per peak hour. This could be achieved by adding a fourth section to the preferred AEG three-section vehicle, while another increase in capacity could be achieved by raising the peak hour service frequency. The principal constraint on increasing the number of services was at the Chepstow Road roundabout between East Croydon and Sandilands, where there could be a maximum of 29 trams per hour in each direction. With the planned service pattern seeing 22 trams an hour in each direction at this point, there remained scope to increase the initial service level by 32% at this bottleneck.

Signalling of the new system was to be predominantly by 'line of sight' rather than by use of visual signals, a design which the PDG had submitted to Her Majesty's Railway Inspectorate (HMRI) without objection. Tram drivers would make decisions on whether to proceed within the limits of a rule book and speed restrictions shown on lineside boards. This was to allow the driver to adapt the speed of his vehicle to the prevailing circumstances, particularly in

The first tram in the fleet (2530) on test at the Bombardier plant in Vienna on 1 September 1998.
(Photo: Harald A. Jahn)

Before delivery to Croydon, 2533 appears at the NEC on 1 November 1998.

the street-running sections of the system. Routes would be set automatically by the vehicles, as pre-programmed by the driver, with localised interlocking at potential conflict points, such as crossings, junctions and single track sections.

While there was to be a central control function, it would only have a supervisory role, although able to assume the role of 'command centre' in the event of abnormal or emergency situations. Each stop on the system was to be equipped with an antenna picking up data from each tram's unique identification and destination code, with radio links giving direct contact between drivers and central control. At each tram stop there was to be a non-contact data exchange system between vehicle and trackside, allowing identification of vehicle number and its destination.

Power supply at 750V DC would be from local utility suppliers – the system not being deemed sufficiently large to justify its own power generation facility – with the current being supplied to the overhead power lines from eleven sub-stations along the route. These overhead lines would be suspended from adjacent buildings where possible, in order to minimise their visual impact, with supporting masts used in areas away from buildings.

A study into the overhead power supply, undertaken the previous year (1993) by Nico Dekker's Rail Systems Consultants, had indicated a need for Tramlink to have a distinctive aesthetic identity and, while current costings were based on a standard design of pole to support the overhead power lines, the PDG did not expect a 'sensitively designed system' to incur a major cost penalty.

Fare collection was one aspect of the Tramlink project where corners were later cut, in order that costs could be reduced by the winning consortium. In its Base Scheme document, the PDG said revenue protection would be in the hands of roving ticket inspectors and put forward what it described as an 'optimised hybrid approach' to combine the use of ticket vending machines with contactless technology.

This would comprise two smartcard readers/validators in each tram along with a single and fairly simple ticket vending machine (TVM) accepting two or three different coin denominations but not giving change, and printing a limited range of paper tickets with three or four fare selection buttons. In addition, coin machines would be located at the six busiest stations – Croydon Central, East Croydon, West Croydon, Wimbledon, New Addington and Addiscombe.

Updating Tramlink's forecast passenger numbers

While the PDG was working to draw up its base specification ahead of the project being put out to tender in 1995, more work was undertaken on reviewing and validating earlier forecasts of ridership levels. In particular, a consultancy called MVA undertook work on behalf of London Transport during 1993 and 1994 to provide more robust estimates of likely demand and revenue.

Its findings, published in a document for London Transport entitled 'Croydon Tramlink – Demand Update' dated September 1995, increased earlier forecasts and suggested that by 2011 the system would be carrying 22,200 passengers during the three-hour (7-10 am) weekday morning peak period, which was in excess of the PDG's expectation in its Base Scheme document of 21,025 passengers.

Putting Tramlink out to Tender

Following a third reading of the Croydon Tramlink Bill in the House of Commons in July 1994, Royal Assent for the Croydon Tramlink Act was granted on 21 July 1994. Five months later, in December 1994, Brian Mawhinney, Secretary of State for Transport, announced public funding for both Tramlink and another proposed tram system, the Midland Metro, provided each was progressed under the government's Private Finance Initiative (PFI). Then, on 30 May 1995, a competition to develop Tramlink was formally launched by Steve

Opening day VIP special trams waiting to depart from New Addington on 10 May 2000.
(Photo: Stephen Parascandalo)

Norris, the Transport Minister, with an advert appearing in the *Official Journal of the European Union* to begin the tendering process.

London Transport held a competition for a 99-year concession to design, build, finance, operate and maintain the Tramlink systems. Bids were invited against a Performance Specification produced by London Transport and the powers granted by the Act of Parliament. During the course of the competition, government confirmed the award of £125 million of grant towards the total project cost of around £200 million, which was one of the lowest grants for any of the UK light rail schemes at that time.

There was a two-stage process, with an initial pre-qualification stage, from which a short-list of suitable candidates would be prepared, followed by a detailed second stage, where the winner was expected to be the company or consortium seeking the lowest level of government grant. A total of eight applications in the pre-qualification competition were whittled down to four short-listed consortia:

- *Altram:* John Laing, Ansaldo Transport and Serco
- *Croydon Connect:* Tarmac, AEG, Transdev (the PDG partners)
- *CT Light Rail Group:* GEC, Alstom, John Mowlem, Welsh Water
- *Tramtrack Croydon:* CentreWest Buses, RBS, Sir Robert McAlpine, Amey, Bombardier Eurorail

A winning bidder is chosen

Bids had to be submitted in January 1996, and in April 1996 Tramtrack Croydon Ltd (TCL) was announced as preferred bidder, subject to its working with the promoters to reduce costs to a level that would be acceptable to government. Then on 22 July 1996 Steve Norris announced that the grant money would be made available, subject to the satisfactory conclusion to negotiations. Finally, on 25 November 1996, TCL was awarded a 99-year concession, with the government awarding a grant of £125 million, including a substantial amount for LT to pay for all the statutory works necessary before construction could begin.

TCL won the competition because it required the least government money to be provided. Its six shareholders were: First Group (operators); Bombardier (suppliers and maintainers of vehicles); Amey Corporation and Sir Robert MacAlpine (responsible for construction); Royal Bank of Scotland and 3i plc (financers). All six were required to attend every TCL Board meeting and all had to agree every major decision.

Under the Concession Agreement TCL was awarded all the rights and given the obligation to construct and operate Tramlink. This agreement also set out the division of risks between the parties, with risks transferred to TCL comprising design, construction and commissioning of the system, operation and maintenance of the completed system and ridership and general business risk. LT, meanwhile, retained responsibility for diversion of statutory utilities equipment and the compulsory acquisition of property.

The first opening day VIP special from New Addington arrives at Sandilands on 10 May 2000.
(Photo: Stephen Parascandalo)

Opening day at East Croydon (10 May 2000), where 2542 in Amey livery stands alongside a bus on the soon-to-be-withdrawn X30 service.

Over the following three months various cost-saving measures were agreed, including a cutting back of the line at New Addington from the library to the health centre, replacement of a proposed new tunnel at the top of Gravel Hill by a road crossing, and reduction in the amount of double tracked line on the Wimbledon route. Changes were also made to the ticket machine design, meaning they would no longer be able to magnetically code tickets, and cheaper masts were selected for the overhead electrification.

The construction programme was relatively short in time-scale, as the ability to start generating cash was critical. In the event this consortium took just as long as the other bidders would have taken, with opening in 2000, a year later than the target of 1999, and meaning that it was four years from award of the contract to operations beginning.

At the time TCL won the concession, demand forecasts suggested that Tramlink would attract 25 million passengers per annum, being used for a wide range of journeys, to the town centres of Croydon and Wimbledon, for employment,

shopping and leisure purposes and via the connections with the National Rail and Underground services to other destinations, particularly central London. Changes to local bus services in the area would provide an integrated network of feeder and complementary services, which would be adjusted in response to the actual changes in demand following the opening of the system. It was estimated that around 10% of Tramlink users would be people transferring from cars.

Construction

Besides Scott McIntosh, another individual to play a key role in the Tramlink story was Phil Hewitt, now heading up the team running the fast-expanding Midland Metro in Birmingham. He joined the project in January 1997 as Engineering Manager, where he oversaw construction and the all-important diversion of utilities, later becoming Project Manager, Tramlink, for TfL in 2001. He then became a key figure in the complex and challenging process of ending the TCL concession

A banner on display at Sandilands announcing the start of Tramlink services.

and the takeover by TfL in 2008, before spending three years as Director, London Tramlink, post the takeover (June 2008 to December 2011).

Speaking to me at his Birmingham office in June 2018, Hewitt explained how it all began in Croydon: 'I joined in January 1997, as part of the project team in an engineering manager role, with a particular focus on managing the utilities diversions. I'd been doing that with London Underground in previous jobs, and that was a really interesting role at the start of the project. The utilities risk was taken by London Transport, and effectively LT had agreed, as part of the tendering process, a programme of utilities diversions that would lead to handover of an allegedly clear corridor to the TCL consortium at specific milestones.

'They could then come in behind us and do the track construction and installation of overhead lines. I have to say that went remarkably well, we built over a period of months an exceptionally good working relationship with Croydon Council – as the highway authority and co-ordinator of what access people had, where and when. We had a really good traffic management meeting to look at those arrangements and to plan and agree what to do when things went wrong, as inevitably they did, when deadlines were not met.

'Allied to that we had a very good relationship with the utility companies and with the construction joint venture, looking at how we would deal with the actual phasing of works and any clashes between the utilities works and the construction works. Broadly that was overall a fifteen-month schedule of work to be undertaken and pretty much it was delivered on time and came in under budget.

'That was a reflection of the sheer amount of planning that had gone in, both by LT and in partnership with TCL, before construction was started and contracts signed, to make sure there was absolute clarity about what was expected and who was going to do what, where and when. That made a huge difference to the deliverability. There were inevitably some difficulties along the way and some areas were handed over slightly late, but broadly without impacting on the construction programme.

'The utilities companies were variable in terms of their relationships – I had at least one interesting conversation with my boss in the pub one evening, when he said he wanted to have a chat – the next thing I knew I was sat in Thames Water's offices for a couple of months working hands-on with their planners and engineers to help them get through the sheer volume of

The Mayors of Sutton and Wimbledon join Bob Dorey, Chairman of TCL, to celebrate the first tram from Wimbledon on 30 May 2000. (Photo: Stephen Parascandalo)

The VIP opening day special tram makes a photo-stop at Phipps Bridge on 30 May 2000. (Photo: Stephen Parascandalo)

what they had to do and coordinate that with the rest of the project, so that was an interesting experience!

'Utilities diversions were principally in Croydon town centre, but also at some of the road crossings on the Wimbledon branch, where there were some pretty hefty water mains in the Merton Park area that needed replacing. At Kent Gate Way on the New Addington line and quite a few sections in Addington Hills there were some interesting cables running through the woods.

'It was a massive coordination and planning exercise – I wouldn't underestimate the sheer amount of work that the Turner & Townsend (T&T) project management team had to do to actually make sure that people were on site doing the right things at the right time with the utility companies. But everybody bought into a process and, as a result of that, it was well-coordinated.

'T&T were also acting as planning supervisor and principal contractor for us on that, so rather than having one utility company after another we had T&T take on that role to coordinate from a safety perspective who was working where and when. There are some bits of Croydon

where the utility diversions became quite material – down Addiscombe Road and Church Street the sewer re-laying was mostly done by ex-miners and was all done in headings and shafts and re-laid in hand-built tunnels under the streets, which was quite a massive undertaking on some of those sections.

'Under the Croydon Tramlink Act, if utilities companies believed they needed to remove their utilities out of the way of our infrastructure, they got to do that, it was their call. But equally, because it was a PFI project, the concessionaire wanted no utilities left and a completely clear corridor where there was no risk of a utility company in the future saying "we need to dig the track up to repair our water main".

'Some crossings were very shallow, and we did have to modify the track design at George Street East, some in George Street West, some at Kent Gate Way, where we simply could not, or could not afford, to move the utilities, so we modified the track design to accommodate leaving things in situ. Actually, that worked very well – we had a process for doing that and then it was worked through and there was no real issue.'

Track installation

'From the utilities work, my role evolved into being the engineering project manager, overseeing the compliance. Nico [Dekker] was one of the people involved in reviewing and advising on the acceptability of the designs and we had a panel of consultants providing us with that input. The process itself went reasonably well – there were a number of challenges with the design and delivery of the infrastructure, but it is worth remembering that this was only the third light rail scheme to be developed in the UK, so we were in new territory and nobody had done one twice.

'The good news was that the Amey McAlpine joint venture did bring down some people with experience of Sheffield Supertram, who had good hands-on experience of building that system and

A ceremonial cutting of the ribbon at the Therapia Lane staff halt on 30 May 2000 to celebrate the start of Wimbledon services. (Photo: Stephen Parascandalo)

Crowds gather around HRH Prince Charles as he pays a visit to Tramlink on 9 December 2000.

who knew what worked and what didn't work and that did mean we were able to evolve a lot of the design work, learning lessons from the Sheffield scheme, in the same way that the operator had brought in a lot of people from Manchester, so we were able to learn from Manchester Metro in the planning of operations.

'Long linear work-sites of the type we had in Croydon are very difficult things to build and having now done a few of them, it is one of the most difficult jobs that a civil engineering firm can undertake.

'It looks like it should be quite straightforward, it's not a deep construction, it's not a complicated construction in theory, but the logistics of how you manage that in an urban environment in a situation where you are right outside people's front doors is one of the most difficult things you can face. You have to carefully coordinate everything and think about the project management, making sure the right things are done in exactly the right sequence.

'Project management is always a challenge in constructing a tramway and Croydon suffered the same sort of problems – planning, as in town & country planning. It is a major challenge, and probably something that was not properly appreciated at the time, managing and being efficient in delivery of planning consents. I don't think anyone really knew what needed to be done and how to make it work, so it was a lot of evolution.

'In terms of quality of construction, there were some issues and we did pick up some things as they were being built. But in terms of the overall quality of the finished product, I would have said it was pretty good for the time. Some of the track-work on the Wimbledon line, where it was re-using the old BR track, was not 100% ideal, but you have to remember that the project was being built for a fairly competitive price.

'A lot of the rail was perfectly serviceable – it was old, but the reality was that it was a PFI and we were working to a price, the team had to make it work as efficiently as they could. The contractors were on a fixed price, so inevitably there is a trade-off in terms of what you are going to get.

'My overall impression is that the construction at the time seemed reasonable – we knew there were some challenges and some issues with it, but it was the concessionaire's risk, so to a degree, as the client, while we might raise our concerns, if the PFI team decided they weren't going to do anything about it, they took all risk on construction, took all fare-box risk and had a 99-year concession, so in theory we weren't that fussed. We would raise issues, challenge them, but if they were going to take that risk, that was their call, it was very pure PFI in that respect.

'As with pretty much every scheme we build in the UK, people say they can build it in three years and take 3½ years – Croydon was much the same. There was some inefficiency in delivery, and there were some legitimate reasons why it was delayed. But relationships with TCL through the construction phase were actually quite positive and we worked well together. There were contractual challenges, but that is the nature of the industry. The LT/TCL relationship was good, professional and worked well.'

Delayed opening but early success

Vital to the successful launch of Tramlink was TCL's ability to secure reliable rolling stock. While issues subsequently arose regarding the quality of its rail infrastructure, there is no doubting that the initial fleet of Bombardier trams have proved extremely reliable over the system's first two decades in operation, and more so than the later order of twelve more technologically-complex Variobahn vehicles from Stadler.

Under the terms of the PFI concession TCL was free to decide on the level of passenger capacity in each vehicle, provided that 30% of passenger capacity was seating, that they were accessible by wheelchairs with two dedicated wheelchair spaces, and did not exceed 45 metres in length. To meet this specification, Bombardier offered a design called CR4000, which was a variant of its K4000 articulated tram, which it had been supplying to Cologne's Stadtbahn from its Vienna plant since 1995.

A Routemaster bus is drafted in to replace Tramlink services following a de-wiring incident on 31 August 2000.
(Photo: Graham Chamberlain)

The 24-strong CR4000 fleet comprises vehicles that are 30.1m long and 2.65m wide, with seats for 70 passengers and standing room for a further 138. They have four doors on each side that are accessible by wheelchair users and baby buggies, being just 350mm above rail height, drawing electric power at 750v DC from the overhead wires and having a maximum speed of 50mph (80km/h).

A number of changes were made to the Cologne design for use in the UK, with seats in the centre articulated section in preference to ticket machines in the Cologne vehicles. In a nice historic touch, the Bombardier fleet was numbered as a continuation from the original London Transport tram numbering system in a sequence from 2530 to 2553, half a century after LT's final tram (2529) had been scrapped.

Delivery of the trams began with the arrival of 2530 at the Therapia Lane depot on 14 September 1998 and continued at a rate of one a week until the final delivery of 2553 on 7 June 1999. The four-day journey of each tram would see it leave Vienna on a Friday evening and be parked in Frankfurt during Saturday. It would then be carried overnight Saturday to the Dutch port of Vlissingen. From here it travelled on a freight ferry to Dartford and parked-up at the port on Sunday night. During Monday mornings they would travel around the M25 to the Clacket Lane service area at Westerham arriving around midday, then park-up until around 19.00.

They would then, with a police escort, consisting of a Range Rover front and rear, patrol car and a helicopter overhead, travel via the M25, M23 and A23 up to the Purley Way, then Ampere Way to the depot. The lorry would enter the depot at around 20.30 each Monday from the Beddington Farm Road roundabout, pull over and straddle the No.1 track on the concrete apron outside the east workshop doors, where each took around ninety minutes to unload. Each arriving tram would remain for about a week in the workshop to be checked over and have safety equipment

fitted, then brake tested on the track between Therapia Lane and Wandle Park before commissioning and running in.

A historic day for the fledgling system came on 8 October 1998 with the very first running of a tram on the system, when 2530 (at the time unnumbered) ventured out for slow speed testing near the Therapia Lane depot. Equally momentous was the first run through the streets of central Croydon on 16 June 1999, when 2535 performed the first powered run on the system's street sections, escorted by four police motorcycles. Given this historic role, 2535 was later named *Stephen Parascandolo*, in honour of the founder of the unofficial Croydon Tramlink website, who was tragically killed in a road accident in 2007 at the age of 26.

Tram Commissioning and Maintenance

Bombardier Transportation not only built the initial tram fleet, but was also contracted to manage its maintenance. Fleet Manager Neil Ambrose of Bombardier, who had been instrumental in the development of a tram maintenance

Sporting the livery of TCL partner Amey, 2542 approaches Waddon Marsh on 13 October 2001 with a Line 1 service to Elmers End. (Photo: Stephen Parascandalo)

Defacing station name boards was an early example of vandalism on Tramlink, where Addiscombe became 'disco' and Waddon Marsh became 'Wad on Mars'.

A ticket issued for travel on a special Tramlink service marking 100 years since the first electric trams reached Croydon.

contract, recruited David Fitzsimmons as Depot Manager from the nearby Network SouthEast depot at Selhurst. David then built his team of multi-skilled technicians by luring four of his Selhurst staff and another three ex-Selhurst colleagues.

This new team was then trained, both in-house and at the manufacturers' location in Austria, Germany and Belgium. Another early recruit was Frank Wilton, who as a consultant was employed to draw up safety and quality depot operating procedures to comply with industry standards. These were subjected to external audit compliance before operational running. During the vehicles' warranty period, engineers from Bombardier in Vienna and Bruges, and from Kiepe Electric, remained on site, carrying out modifications alongside the in-house maintenance team.

As the system infrastructure was being completed and audited the newly-delivered trams were run to accumulate fault-free mileage before they could be released for service. Loaded operational testing was carried out by filling the empty trams with sandbags or crane weights, to simulate crush loaded operation on the steep gradients. One early technical problem was wheel wear, which was ameliorated by TCL fitting track lubricators at severe wear points and fitting flange lubricators to the trams.

Tram Stops

The tram stops have low platforms, 35cm (14in) above rail level. They are unstaffed and were equipped with automated ticket machines (taken out of use in July 2018). In general, access between the platforms involves crossing the tracks by pedestrian level crossing. There are now 39 stops, most being 32.2m (106ft) long. They are virtually level with the doors, which allows wheelchairs, prams, pushchairs and the elderly to board the tram easily with no steps. In street sections, the stop is integrated with the pavement.

On sections of the network where Tramlink served former railway stations between Wimbledon and West Croydon and between Elmers End and Coombe Lane, railway platforms were demolished and rebuilt at the lower height required by Tramlink. Two exceptions were Elmers End and Wimbledon, where the track level was raised to meet the higher main-line platforms to enable cross-platform interchange.

A total of thirty-eight stops opened in the initial phased introduction of tram services during May 2000, with one additional town centre stop, Centrale, opening after much wrangling on 10 December 2005 (see below) and increasing journey times slightly. All stops have disabled access, raised paving, CCTV, a Passenger Help Point, a Passenger Information Display (PID), litter bins, a noticeboard and lamp-posts, and most also have seats and a shelter. The PIDs display the destinations and expected arrival times of the next two trams and can be used to display information on delays to the service.

THE CROYDON CENTENARIAN

Celebrating the opening of Croydon's first electric tramway on 26th September 1901

Admit one passenger to the Special Tram leaving East Croydon Station at 10.25 am for a tour of the Tramlink system

Sunday 23rd September 2001

The tour will end at Church Street at around 1.30 pm, followed by an elegant collation at the *Dog and Bull* public house in Surrey Street

1901-2001

Services begin

After many weeks of false dawns, Tramlink was finally opened to passengers in three stages during May 2000. Most fanfare was made when services began between Croydon and New Addington (Route 3) on 10 May 2000, with rather lesser events taking place to mark the start of services to Beckenham Junction (Route 2) on 23 May and finally one week later (30 May) between Wimbledon and Elmers End (Route 1).

Events on Wednesday, 10 May, began with invited guests being taken to New Addington aboard two buses, where there were speeches and a ceremonial ribbon-cutting before guests boarded trams 2543 and 2550. These were adorned with wreaths of flowers on the front and left New Addington for Croydon at around 12.30. Later in the day 2543 worked the first public departure from New Addington, at around 13.00, while 2550 operated the first public service from Croydon to New Addington – all services on the opening day being free, and therefore very busy.

The launch day press announcement from TCL was headed 'London's trams are back – with help from 1950s driver' and explained how 82-year-old Fred Roberts, who had driven one of the last Croydon trams back in 1951, would 'be close to the driving seat' when the first of London's new trams started carrying passengers on 10 May. He joined the Mayor of Croydon, Dr Shafi Khan, in opening the first phase of Tramlink, along with some of the key figures who had helped develop the project over the previous decade and dozens of community representatives.

Commenting on the launch, TCL chairman Bob Dorey said: 'We are absolutely delighted to be opening for public service. It has been important to get everything right for launching a safe and reliable service and now we can

An early instance of a road traffic accident on 10 March 2001, where 2533 in Nescafé livery has hit a car in Wellesley Road. (Photo: Stephen Parascandalo)

start demonstrating what the latest state-of-the-art public transport can do for passengers in south London. I particularly want to pay personal tribute to Croydon Council and London Transport for having the vision to promote Tramlink and, to London Transport for arranging the concession to build and operate the system.'

In response, Clive Hodson, LT Project Director with responsibility for Tramlink declared, 'I am delighted that the first stage of Tramlink is opening today and I am quite sure it will be a huge success in this important part of London. It will provide fast, fully accessible journeys and will be crucial to persuading people out of their cars and on to public transport. The key to its success will be its integration with bus services, including the dedicated Tramlink feeder services, the National Rail network and the Underground. It is a fine illustration of what can be achieved when central and local government, transport authorities and the private sector act together in partnership.'

Finally, Croydon Council leader Hugh Malyan added his endorsement of the new system: 'Already there are encouraging signs that Tramlink is becoming a catalyst for new economic investment as well

as being a vivid symbol of confidence in Croydon's progress at the start of the millennium. The extensive green landscaping that has grown up as the tram route has been built is brightening the appearance of the borough and, in the central area, the trams have added to the colourful continental feel of the place with its busy pavement cafés and buzzing atmosphere.'

To coincide with Tramlink's opening, two feeder bus services began running from New Addington to Addington Village Interchange on Thursday, 11 May, the first full day of tram operation. Route T31 ran from Vulcan Way via King Henry's Drive, Homestead Way, Overbury Crescent, Parkway, King Henry's Drive, Goldcrest Way, Headley Drive, Merrow Way, Fieldway and Lodge Lane. The second new service, Route T32, ran from the New Addington (Parkway) Tram Stop via Central Parade, Arnhem Drive, King Henry's Drive, Goldcrest Way, Headley Drive and Lodge Lane.

Through single tickets would be available for transfer to and from the trams at no extra charge for the bus journey. Meanwhile, another significant change to the local public transport network was withdrawal of the Express bus X30 from New Addington to West Croydon, which ceased after 10 May. In a further change, from 20 May feeder bus T31 was extended to Forestdale, Courtwood Lane, to coincide with other bus service changes in the Addington area. Another change was launch of a third feeder route, the T33 (Addington Village–Selsdon Vale–Selsdon). As the system-opening publicity leaflet noted, all the new feeder routes would be run with brand new low-floor and wheelchair-accessible single deck buses.

Almost two weeks after the grand New Addington opening, the Beckenham Junction line opening on Tuesday, 23 May 2000, was a low key affair. At 10.45 the leader of Bromley Council cut the ribbon after making a short speech in which he wished the line success and also said that a feasibility study was underway into

Severe winter weather in Croydon as 2542 heads away from East Croydon towards central Croydon on 8 January 2003. (Photo: Stephen Parascandalo)

Track renewal work
at West Croydon
on 30 May 2005.
(Photo: John Kaye)

extending to Crystal Palace. Tram 2548 then took invited guests to Croydon and back before forming the first public service, the 12.02 departure from Beckenham Junction. No free travel was offered on this occasion and many of those travelling on that first journey were tram enthusiasts.

One week on from the Beckenham Junction opening, inauguration of Route 1 from Wimbledon to Elmers End took place in virtual secrecy on Tuesday, 30 May 2000. A small group of VIPs gathered at the staff halt outside Therapia Lane depot where a ribbon was cut and the VIPs then travelled on tram 2548 to Wimbledon, stopping at Phipps Bridge for photos. After the VIPs had returned to Croydon, public services began at 12.00, with the first departure from Wimbledon formed by tram 2538, which was packed with enthusiasts and others when it left at midday. Opening of

the route to trams was almost exactly three years since the last passenger train had run on 31 May 1997.

Initial day-time frequencies (07.00–19.00 on Mondays to Saturdays) were services every 12 minutes on Routes 1 and 2, with a service every 7 minutes on Route 3 to New Addington. Fares at opening were 90p for any journey from Beckenham Junction, Elmers End or New Addington to Central Croydon and as far as what was then the Zone 3 boundary at Merton Park, with fares that crossed the Zone 3 boundary, such as those to and from Wimbledon, costing £1.30. These fares included any connecting journey on the three new Addington bus routes at no extra cost. Travelcards for Zones 4, 5 or 6 could be used anywhere on Tramlink, except between Merton Park and Wimbledon, where Zone 3 validity was required.

Positive early reaction to Tramlink

As the man responsible for its original promotion and development, Scott McIntosh fondly recalls how Tramlink quickly became popular among Croydon residents: 'I remember during the first weeks that Tramlink was running I was standing on the stop at Lebanon Road waiting to go into Croydon and one of the other passengers turned to me and said, "Isn't it wonderful that this has got in here, this road used to be so noisy in the morning, but now I can hear the birds singing." Then a bus went past and she added, "apart from those bloody buses!".'

McIntosh added that in those first few years of Tramlink operations people in Croydon were saying things like 'we feel quite Continental now, we can hear the tram bells ringing and we have cleaner and brighter streets.' He points out that the system had heralded urban improvements, such as the area in front of East Croydon station, which had been a mess for years. 'They got a new station building and then we gave them a nice forecourt. I think those things were very important in showing the people that there were a lot of upsides on the project, despite the construction phase having

been handled badly and annoying a large number of people.

'One thing we did, which was partly a trick I had learned in Sheffield, was that the Council took one of their retired rating officers and they set him up in offices next to the Library, so it was not obviously Council. Anybody who lived in the Borough, particularly the business community, who felt that their business had been damaged by construction of the tramway, could come to him, and the promise was that he would examine their case and, if he thought that they had a case to make, he would assist them in making a case to his former employer for a reduction in their rates. In three years, not one person made a sustainable case, but none of them was turned away without a hearing.'

On 5 December 2000, Tramlink was honoured by a visit from Prince Charles, who arrived at East Croydon at around 13.15 and met the crowds of well-wishers, before boarding tram 2549 to take him to New Addington. The tram had been specially cleaned and waxed, with any scratched glass film replaced. Bombardier fitters had also modified the wing mirror to enable the Royal Pennant to be fitted to the tram. At Addington Village the tram picked up some disabled people and

A driver's eye view of the Wandle flyover and central Croydon. (Photo: Stephen Parascandalo)

Another driver's eye view – this time of the descent from Wandle flyover towards Waddon New Road.

parents with buggies and for part of the journey the Prince travelled in the cab next to the driver.

A successful first year

For all the issues over revenues that would dog TCL throughout its eight-year custodianship of Tramlink, there was no doubting its early success. Management had declared its aim of achieving twenty million passenger journeys a year and removing two million car journeys a year from Croydon's roads after three years of operation. Figures published in May 2001 recorded between 50,000 and 60,000 journeys a day. The service was also reliable – more than 99% of scheduled kms being operated, and correct headways, that is the time between each tram, achieved 98.6% of the time.

Reaping the benefits of Tramlink's popularity, the Whitgift Shopping Centre in Croydon reported a 9% increase in footfall since the system opened, with an even bigger increase of 15% over the Christmas period, when there had also been a 7% reduction in car parking. In Croydon town centre a pavement café culture was starting to develop in George Street, while Tramlink was seen as a catalyst for regeneration, with a number of major redevelopment schemes underway, including the Centrale shopping centre and a new Multiplex cinema and leisure complex.

Creating a favourable impact

Two years after the system's opening, a study undertaken by TfL and the Department for Transport (*Croydon Tramlink Impact Study*, June 2002) assessed

Another tram that carried an all-over advertising livery was 2546, promoting the Whitgift Shopping Centre, seen here arriving at Mitcham Junction on 10 June 2000. (Photo: Stephen Parascandalo)

its impact through surveys carried out both before Tramlink opened (September 1999 to March 2000) and after (December 2000 to December 2001). At this early stage in the system's history, ridership had reached 17.3m in the year to September 2001, with significantly more female (58%) than male (42%) passengers.

In terms of age profile, the study showed that it was being least used by people under 25 (14% of total ridership), with the heaviest users being in the 45 to 59-year-old band (24% of total ridership). Journeys to work accounted for the highest proportion of trips (44%), with shopping (26%) being the second most common journey purpose. Tramlink had quickly established itself as a regular travel choice, with more than half of respondents to the survey (53%) saying that they travelled more than four times a week on it, and a further 21% travelling by tram 2-3 times a week.

One of the key measures of Tramlink's appeal was the extent to which it could achieve that holy grail of transport planners, modal shift, i.e. getting people out of their cars. Here the 2002 study was very positive, showing that Tramlink had captured 15% of all weekday trips being made by people living within 800m of a tram stop, and even more at weekends (17%). Most impressive of all was the modal split for New Addington, where Tramlink accounted for 32% of all trips, the highest of any single mode, on weekdays, while car usage had dropped from 59% to 32% on weekdays and from 72% to 41% at weekends.

Although the vast majority of those switching to Tramlink were previously bus users (69%), 7,000 car journeys per day had also made the switch (16% of the total), with 22% of respondents now making journeys they had not previously undertaken. Of those who had changed mode to tram, 55% had a car available and 86% had an alternative mode of transport available, showing the high proportion of passengers who were opting for Tramlink in preference to other modes, including the car.

By far the most striking transformation brought about by Tramlink could be seen along the Wimbledon–Croydon corridor, whose 'Cinderella' rail service had closed in May 1997, although rail replacement buses had then operated until Tramlink's opening. The 2002 study noted that between 1994 and 2001 the introduction of high frequency light rail services had led to an eightfold increase in patronage during the morning peak period. In the case of stations, such as Mitcham Junction, served by both national rail and Tramlink, the increase was between five and six times, during a period (1994-2001) when the number of rail passengers entering central London during the morning peak period had risen by a rather more modest 13%.

Other key findings of the 2002 Impact Study were a reduction in demand for off-street car parking, with overall entries into publicly-owned off-street car parks down by 6% in the twelve months after Tramlink opened. Comparing responses to the 'before' survey with those given once the system had opened, 56% of respondents said that they were actually using Tramlink more than they had expected before its opening, with only 17%

saying that they were using it less than expected. Principal reasons given for using the system more than expected were that it was reliable, fast and frequent.

A wide range of positive comments was unearthed by the study. Pre-opening fears that the system would lead to accidents or that broken down trams would create 'gridlock' proved unfounded, press coverage had become more positive and some car drivers noted that their journey times had been reduced. Estate agents reported increased house prices in areas made more accessible by Tramlink, while users and non-users alike expressed the view that the system had been a good thing for Croydon, making it 'The London Borough with the Tram'. Perceptions of buses in Croydon did not alter significantly between the before and after surveys, but respondents' perceptions of trams did improve for a range of attributes including ride quality, feeling of safety and journey time. In other words, reality proved better than expectation.

A first ever strike hits Tramlink

But it was not all plain sailing for TCL in the early honeymoon period of its regime. On 26 March 2002 Tramlink experienced its first ever strike, with workers threatening a series of walkouts over pay. Drivers belonging to the Transport and General Workers' Union (TGWU) were demanding the same pay as colleagues on London's buses and Tube, but TCL said it could not afford the wage hike and it offered arbitration to try to come to a deal. Croydon tram drivers, who were earning about £17,000 a year for a 40-hour week, voted overwhelmingly to strike, and on the day of the strike trams only ran between East Croydon and Wimbledon, with replacement buses on other routes.

The first member of the fleet (2530) stands in evening sunshine at Therapia Lane on 12 June 2004 with a service to Wimbledon. (Photo: Stephen Parascandalo)

More tram networks for London?

Such was the success of Tramlink that plans for tram schemes elsewhere in the capital soon emerged. On 29 May 2002 the *Evening Standard* reported the unveiling of a £500m plan that would see trams return to the streets of central London for the first time in fifty years. Mayor Ken Livingstone had given the go-ahead for the £300m north-south Cross River link, championed by Scott McIntosh during his time at LT, as well as a £200m tramway through west London. The West London tram, due to be completed by 2009, would run from Uxbridge to Shepherds Bush via Acton, Ealing, Hanwell and Southall town centres. The Cross River tram, due for completion by 2011, would link Camden and Kings Cross, via Euston and Waterloo, to Peckham and Brixton in the south.

Livingstone made the announcement to complement his controversial introduction of congestion charging in central London, a move which he hoped would see passengers switch from car to tram, following the success of Tramlink in Croydon: 'The West London and Cross River Trams will provide faster and more reliable public transport in these heavily congested areas of London,' he declared. 'I will be talking to the government about how to speed up the planning process which would enable these schemes to be delivered even more rapidly.' Up to 122 million passengers each year were expected to use the new networks, with 72 million passengers on the Cross River tram and 50 million in West London.

Demonstrating his enthusiasm for trams, Livingstone paid a visit to Croydon on 30 January 2003, less than a week before the first signs of financial stress at TCL began to emerge. He boarded at the George Street stop and travelled to the Therapia Lane depot, where he met Managing Director John Rymer and members of staff. He later continued to Mitcham Junction by tram and, in speeches during his tour, made positive comments about the prospects for Tramlink extensions to Crystal Palace and from Sutton to Tooting. Asked by the *Croydon Advertiser*

A Line 1 service from Wimbledon to Elmers End approaches Wandle Bridges on 28 December 2000. (Photo: Stephen Parascandalo)

if he believed Croydon provided a model for the rest of London, Livingstone replied, 'Yes, I think the Croydon Tramlink has been extremely successful and I am keen to bring in other similar schemes across London.'

The economic benefits of Tramlink

A further study into the impact of Tramlink, this time by consultants Colin Buchanan and Partners and published in August 2003, revealed the range of benefits that the system had brought to Croydon and the surrounding areas. It was commissioned by the South London Partnership, a body comprising local authorities and business, and more than 100 businesses, community groups and individuals were interviewed. Among its key conclusions was that businesses in Croydon have had their profiles raised by Tramlink, increasing customer numbers and business activity.

The accessibility of the tram system had been an important factor in attracting new firms into the area, said the report, making it easier for companies to recruit and retain staff, with some reporting that the punctual trams meant staff no longer had any excuse for being late for work. There had also been a dramatic drop in unemployment since Tramlink services began, while house prices along the tram routes had risen faster than in other parts of the borough and properties near to Tramlink were proving easier to sell.

'It is evident that Croydon has seized the opportunity presented by Tramlink for new investment, to raise its profile and to bring a sense of panache and buzz to its centre,' concluded the report.

An editorial comment in the *Croydon Advertiser* entitled 'Confirmation if needed of tram benefits' praised the report's upbeat conclusions: 'It is satisfying to read the survey which shows the reality is exactly the opposite [of the predicted gloom]. Success goes even wider; unemployment levels in areas close to the route have dropped more than in areas away from it and houses with Tramlink in their sights have become very saleable. With that kind of good news under its belt, we look forward to Transport for London having the courage and the cash to extend the system and bring benefits to even more people and businesses.'

2535 stands at Phipps Bridge stop on 28 December 2000 with a curtailed Line 1 service. (Photo: Stephen Parascandalo)

CHAPTER 5

FINANCIAL MELTDOWN AT TCL

Having first run into difficulties in late 2001, by the start of 2003 Tramlink concessionaire TCL was in serious financial trouble. Even before its problems were exacerbated by sweeping fares reforms that were announced later in the year, it was clear that TCL faced fundamental difficulties. Its revenue forecasts had proved to be grossly over-optimistic, while operation of the network took about eighteen months to get to a point where it was operating the level of service that was originally forecast. Under the terms of its concession, LT underwrote a number of fares risks, but TCL took the demand risk, so if TCL over-estimated demand, and demand fell short,

then it would not be compensated for any demand (passengers) it had not carried.

One month into the year and TCL's parlous financial position became starkly apparent on 5 February 2003. Extensive national media reports gave details of its serious financial problems, with filings at Companies House indicating that, at the time its Annual Accounts for the year to 31 March 2002 had been prepared, TCL had insufficient funds to continue trading beyond 25 March 2003. While ridership reached 18.2m in the year 2001/2, TCL incurred a 34% increase in its pre-tax loss to £9.47 million for the year to 31 March 2002, with operating losses more than doubling to £1.58 million.

One vehicle of 2551 sports an advertising livery on 16 March 2005 as it stands at East Croydon with a Line 3 service to New Addington.
(Photo: Gareth Prior)

The business was weighed down by net debts of more than £100m, with its accounts suggesting that refinancing discussions were underway and indicating that there was 'a realistic prospect' of interim funding if a refinancing deal was not agreed in the next few weeks. One investment analyst commented: 'It's difficult to see how TCL will ever make money. It doesn't break even at the operating level, so how can it pay down debt of more than £100 million?' Another said its position underlined the need for greater transparency in the accounting of special purpose vehicles (SPVs), the name for the financially-engineered entities like TCL used to deliver PFI projects.

In its report on the financial crisis, BBC News noted that it would come as a blow for Transport for London, which had formed a special division to oversee the development of trams in the capital, and for struggling infrastructure firm Amey, which led the consortium to build and run Tramlink. The crisis would also add further doubts about how the Private Finance Initiative secured the involvement of

private firms in construction and operation of public sector programmes, and had also been used in hospital, prison and school projects. An Amey spokeswoman told the BBC that, in the case of the Tramtrack crisis, it was private sector companies that stood to pick up the tab. 'It is the private sector which is exposed to the risk,' she said.

Only days before the exposure of TCL's financial woes, a National Audit Office report had said PFI had delivered 'dramatic improvement', completing projects with fewer delays and cost overruns. But pointers to the problems at TCL could be seen in some early rejigging of its shareholding structure. In 2002 FirstGroup, one of Tramtrack's original shareholders, and still operator of the system, sold its interest, and in 2001 Amey had sold down half of its interest in Tramlink for a nominal £5,000 to Actio, a Jersey-based firm. When construction group John Laing bought a £29.1m portfolio of PFI projects from Amey in January 2003, Tramlink was excluded from the deal, with John Laing chairman Bill Forrester dismissing Tramlink as 'too risky'.

2533 waits at Wimbledon on 1 November 2005 with a Line 1 service to Elmers End.
(Photo: Gareth Prior)

A report in the following day's *Times* (6 February 2003) – 'Tramlink backers get on board for re-finance talks' – said that banks and shareholders backing the heavily indebted Croydon Tramlink were understood to be considering a debt-for-equity swap in an effort to refinance the project ahead of a crucial deadline next month. TCL's shareholders included Amey, a troubled support services group, Sir Robert McAlpine, the construction group, Royal Bank of Scotland and 3i Group, the private equity house. In addition a consortium of banks led by Mizuho Corporate Bank had also provided debt funding for TCL, with representatives of two of the banks backing the project leading the refinancing talks which were said to include a debt-for-equity swap in an effort to cut TCL's debt.

Financial difficulties too at Midland Metro

Tramlink was not alone in being a financially-distressed light rail system that was the product of PFI. One week after TCL's woes became public, *The Times* reported (12 February 2003) that Midland Metro, the tram system that links Birmingham and Wolverhampton, was on the brink of financial collapse after auditors refused to sign off the accounts of the company formed to build and run the system, a consortium called Altram LRT, which included John Laing and National Express.

Altram LRT accounts for the year to 31 December 2001 showed a pre-tax loss of £11.4 million in 2001, on turnover of £4.32 million, and said that its future was

New trams for Nottingham were tested on Tramlink, as seen at Blackhorse Lane on 31 March 2003. (Photo: Stephen Parascandalo)

2548 stops at
Woodside on
1 November 2005
with a Line 1 service
to Elmers End.
(Photo: Gareth Prior)

dependent on restructuring talks with Centro, the West Midlands transport authority: 'Since the year end, the company has been in negotiation with Centro regarding a new performance regime and financial restructuring, successful completion of which will enable the company to trade for the foreseeable future.' Once again it raised concerns from analysts of the listed constituent companies about the lack of disclosure of PFI projects in those parent companies' accounts.

Days after the widespread coverage of its financial difficulties, TCL was able to confirm that tram services would continue unaffected, with the situation having not come as a surprise to senior managers, and measures already being taken to resolve the problems. In an interview with the *Croydon Guardian*, Roger Harding, TCL General Manager, said, 'Our banks have indicated to us that they are working energetically towards refinancing, but that if they don't find it, they could see how they could accommodate some

interim refinancing in order to tide us over.' Arrangements between TCL and TfL would always ensure that the trams continued operating.

In a further comment on the financial crisis, shortly after the 25 March 2003 deadline had passed, Harding outlined the consortium's financial situation to the London Transport Users' Committee. He pointed out that, contrary to the press speculation a few weeks before, Tramlink did not stop operating on 25 March. Agreement had been reached with its bankers for an Interim Funding arrangement, pending refinancing. TCL was confident the matter would be resolved and said there was no possibility of Tramlink ceasing to operate and now 'very little possibility' of TCL not remaining the Tramlink concessionaire.

Major partner Amey was less optimistic however, and wrote down the value of its TCL investment. In its 2002 Annual Report (published on 31 March 2003), newly-appointed Chief Executive Mel Ewell noted that TCL, in which it held a 50% stake, was one of two group investments (the other being a wireless technology business called BCN) which 'continued to demonstrate uncertain future investment returns'. He went on to add, 'Our response has been to cease further investment at Croydon, which is now effectively in control of its bankers.' In its Financial Review, the 2002 Amey Annual Report says that the stake in TCL was being written down to just £3.9m, 'being the amount of an anticipated insurance recovery' – so effectively nothing – and was due to its (TCL's) 'poor trading'.

A fares revolution and demand takes off

Having started operations with just two standard adult single fares of 90p or £1.30, as mentioned above, there were a number of subsequent revisions to the fares structure, one of which was to have a profound effect on levels of patronage. This occurred on 4 January 2004, when Tramlink fares were brought into line with those on London Buses by putting the whole system into Zone 4 when a £1.00 flat fare was introduced for all journeys. At the same time the Bus and Tram pass was scrapped and holders of a bus pass could now use Tramlink, along with any travelcard covering any of Zones 3, 4, 5 or 6. Another significant change at this time was the introduction of free travel for under-11-year-olds, who were required to have a photo-card to prove their age.

A further significant change to fares policy in 2004 came with acceptance of Oyster pre- payment cards from 16 May 2004. Once loaded with 'credit' at ticket agents, underground stations or online, these could be used to save 30% of the cash fare when travelling on Tramlink. Card

2537 stands at New Addington on 15 March 2006 with a Line 3 service to West Croydon.
(Photo: Gareth Prior)

Old and new destination displays are evident in this 15 March 2006 view of Addington Village, where 2541 sports a digital display while 2539 retains the original roller blind. (Photo: Gareth Prior)

holders had to touch in on a card reader at the tram stop they were boarding from and the 70p fare would then be deducted from the balance of the holder's credit. The combined effect of these 2004 fare changes saw a huge uplift in passenger numbers on Tramlink, which had grown from 18.7m in 2002/3 to 19.8m in 2003/4, but then surged to 22.0m in 2004/5 as the full effects of these more attractive fares was reflected in traffic levels.

This standardisation of fares to £1 (70p with Oyster) together with the ability to use bus passes on trams also led to increased passenger satisfaction. A TCL survey in February 2004 showed that 84% of passengers 'did not mind the increase'. Passengers had found the 90p and £1.30 fares awkward, as it had meant waiting for change or finding the right money at tram stop ticket machines, whereas it had become much quicker being able to pay with a £1 coin. This resulted in 87% of people saying that they now found it easier to use the ticket machines with a single flat fare.

Reducing the fare from £1.30 led to a particular increase on the Wimbledon line, where more people from areas such as Kingston were travelling to Croydon via Wimbledon. In addition, the ability to use bus passes on Tramlink had led to improved integration and connections with local buses, and reduced the level of ticketless travel. There was a particularly noticeable switch from bus to tram at New Addington, while crowding on the Wimbledon line meant some Tramlink employees were unable to board trams from East Croydon to the Therapia Lane depot between 08.30 and 09.00.

The saga of Centrale

Symptomatic of the strained relationship between TCL and TfL was the issue of a 39th stop on the system, originally expected to be called Tamworth Road but later known as Centrale. This stop appeared in the original designs for Tramlink, and should have opened to passengers on 2 April 2004, to coincide

2544 approaches
Sandilands on
15 March 2006
with a Line 1 service
to Wimbledon.
(Photo: Gareth Prior)

with the opening of the new Centrale shopping centre between Tamworth Road and North End, with shoppers being able to alight outside the centre's main entrance, walk through the centre onto North End and then the Whitgift Centre, before boarding a tram again at the Wellesley Road stop.

Centrale's developers, St. Martin's Property Corporation, had made provision in its retail scheme for the tram stop in Tamworth Road, and Croydon Council negotiated a further contribution to fitting out the tram stop as part of the process of it granting planning permission. But TCL wanted more out of the deal, claiming that stopping 21 trams an hour at Centrale would wreck its timetable, and claimed that an extra tram, enhanced capacity on the Wimbledon line and additional signalling would be needed for it to maintain its contractual obligation to run 21 trams an hour round the Croydon loop.

TCL maintained that at the time it had signed TfL's Tramlink concession and Service Agreement, the system had not opened and that it therefore had no

practical experience of the ability of the system to meet the contractual timetable obligations for service frequency, journey times and service gaps: 'The modelling that we have done suggests that revenue would be significantly undermined if the service performance to each of the current destinations were to deteriorate. Similarly the potential for generation of additional revenue is less clear to us as many passengers alighting at Centrale would already be using other central Croydon stops…this means that with TCL operating reliably, any change which degrades its service performance could worsen the TCL revenue position.'

Responding to a question about Centrale in the London Assembly on 19 September 2005, Mayor Ken Livingstone pointed out that introduction of the new tram stop in Tamworth Road represented the single biggest investment in Tramlink since it opened in 2000: 'The new stop requires changes to the infrastructure of the system and the introduction of a new timetable,' he said. 'The new timetable will itself place a higher level of demand on the existing tram fleet than originally envisaged in 1996 and will in the medium term require an additional tram to ensure the robustness of the service.'

Livingstone said negotiations between TCL and TfL had been taking place over the past ten months, pointing out that whenever a PFI contract is involved negotiations are protracted and have to address many issues associated with the allocation of risk and financial liabilities: 'I am pleased however to be able to confirm that following a meeting between the Head of London Trams and the Managing Director of TCL in mid-August, broad agreement on the scope, cost and risk allocation to deliver this project was reached. Instructions were recently issued to TCL to implement the necessary works.'

After a stand-off that had lasted well over eighteen months, Centrale tram stop finally opened to the public on 10 December 2005. While its opening was to have waited until an additional tram had been purchased, in order to maintain the current service frequency it was opened under the existing timetable but with a new timetable and an extra diagram to begin in the New Year and the new tram originally demanded by TCL still being sought.

TCL takes legal action against TfL

Having finally agreed a vital refinancing package with its banking group in 2004, the long-running dispute between TCL and TfL continued to grow. On 7 January 2005, TCL threatened legal action against TfL, on the basis that changes to fares structures resulted in cheaper bus travel during the early years of operation, leading to the trams appearing more expensive, meaning fewer passengers than expected were using Tramlink. TCL believed that TfL had caused this, and was considering suing to recover some revenue from an estimated eight million passenger shortfall, its position being reinforced by the huge growth in tram passenger numbers that had been seen since bus passes had been allowed on trams as part of the January 2004 fares reforms.

2553 pauses at Sandilands on 15 March 2006 with a Line 1 service to Wimbledon.
(Photo: Gareth Prior)

2535 pauses
at Centrale on
13 September 2006
with a Line 3 service
to New Addington.
(Photo: Gareth Prior)

At the heart of the dispute between the two parties was the question of apportioning risk in the event that revenues fell short of expectations. Under the terms of the 1996 Concession Agreement, LT (TfL) underwrote a number of fares risks under what was called the off-tram revenue agreement, but there were key risks that the concessionaire (TCL) took around inflation of costs and revenue increases, demand risk and various other issues. In the event that there were changes to the regulated fares that TfL operated, such as Travelcards, and if fare increases were capped below the assumed levels in the concession, then there was a mechanism which would compensate TCL for any consequent shortfall in revenues. But TCL took demand risk, so the fares compensation would only ever pay out relative to the level of demand that was actually seen on the network.

Taking up the TCL/TfL dispute in the Greater London Assembly during the January 2005 Mayor's Question Time session, Liberal Democrat Lynne Featherstone raised the matter with Mayor Ken Livingstone by asking him, 'Why has it taken so long for Transport for London to resolve its differences with TCL and how do you expect to retain the confidence of fourteen major financial lenders unless TfL is trusted to uphold the spirit as well as the letter of PFI contracts?'

In his typically robust response, Livingstone acknowledged that TCL had a number of claims against TfL, which it did not believe were justified or likely to succeed: 'TCL felt it necessary to publicise the pursuit of these in the press recently, but balanced reporting by the *Financial Times* pointed out the system was delivered late, delaying revenue income, and that TCL entered into the Concession Agreement on the basis of its own assessment of the risks and potential returns. LRT and subsequently TfL provided limited financial guarantees in respect of a number of the assumptions underpinning TCL's financing plan. Where circumstances required, the guarantees have been met.

'I am confident that in its dealings with TCL, TfL has ensured that it has applied the provisions of the Concession Agreement in a manner that is consistent with both the contractual terms and the risk transfer envisaged when the PFI deal was made in 1996. I do not however consider it appropriate for TfL to settle claims made by the private sector whenever risks willingly accepted for potentially large benefits are realised and without ensuring that it does everything to secure value for money. No provisions are being made in TfL's budget for the current claims as it is not judged they will be successful.'

Under the 1996 Concession Agreement, Retail Price Index (RPI) risk was with the concessionaire, but where TCL had assumed a figure of growth in the RPI figure of 3½% it was actually coming in at 2%. So although TCL was getting an RPI+1% increase in the contribution it received from TfL every year, its over-estimation of future RPI increases meant

that each year there was a shortfall in its revenues, which progressively widened into a fairly hefty gap between forecast and actual revenues. As a result of this increasingly untenable position for both sides, TfL and TCL mutually agreed to invoke the dispute resolution procedure contained in the Concession Agreement and to refer a number of legal arguments to the courts, to fast track the resolution process.

Ending the TCL Concession

Tensions between the two sides were coming to a head by the end of 2005, when TfL Transport Commissioner Peter Hendy expressed concerns over how the state of the system's track and the jaded look of the trams, inside and out, might start to put passengers off. 'We think the physical condition of the system is in decline. Our concern is for the passengers, whereas theirs seems to be for their profitability.'

2538 has just left Lloyd Park stop on 16 October 2006 with a Line 3 service to Wimbledon.
(Photo: Gareth Prior)

Hendy said TfL would be looking closely at how the 99-year concession was working and would not hesitate to default the company if it was seriously unhappy with the set-up. 'That might mean they do not hold the concession for the remainder of the period involved,' he warned.

In an interview at his Birmingham offices (he is now head of Midland Metro), Phil Hewitt, who had become Head of Trams at TfL in April 2004 and oversaw the whole process of terminating TCL's concession, explained why the legal route had been taken to resolve matters between TCL and TfL: 'We needed to understand how we could take the concession forward one way or another, and we had identified that there was a big contractual issue there that was a blocker to either side being able to make decisions on its strategy for the future of the concession.

'The dispute originated as an agreement between us and we had to put that point in front of a Court in order to get a definitive argument that would allow the Mayor and

TfL to go forward and indeed for TCL and its shareholders. From the public sector [TfL] perspective, there was a very clear view that the concessionaire [TCL] had taken on all these [revenue] risks, and if it went bankrupt so be it. And from the concessionaire's [TCL] point of view, there was a feeling that it shouldn't have taken certain risks and it wanted to be bailed out.

'Without a resolution of this key point we would end up deadlocked with one side or the other saying "no". We agreed we would go straight to court, not using the various layers of dispute resolution within the contract [Concession Agreement], because all we wanted was certainty, and the easiest way to get certainty was to go to court. Then both sides constructed their arguments around what was the meaning of the contract and what compensation would be paid for new tickets. TCL was of the view that all new tickets should be compensated at the original cash fare, but clearly that was not what TfL thought was the case. TfL's

2533 approaches
Beddington Lane
on 13 March 2007
with a Line 3 service
to New Addington.
(Photo: Gareth Prior)

position was that if we introduced new tickets there would be a mechanism to maintain the concessionaire's position – no better or no worse.

'We were all looking at options for the future of the concession and how we would fund it. We were looking at the fares compensation formula and how that would work, along with our future budgets. There was no winner or loser position in this – if TCL had won [in court] we would have had to end up terminating the concession and buying them out; if we won, then TCL would need to come to the table and ask for us to buy them out. So the outcome was always going to be the same, it was just the rationale for getting there.

'But it gave us the mechanism to then put in place the outcomes – as it was the argument went in favour of LT/TfL, so it facilitated the discussion within TCL – among its shareholders – and with TfL as to how you then closed down the concession. They [TCL] had

certainty about what their financial prospects looked like – if it had gone the other way, we would have had the same conversation, but it would have been from the perspective that we would have looked at the result and concluded that it [the concession] was no longer affordable.'

Summing up how relations were between TfL and TCL, Hewitt describes the situation as having got quite fractious at times during this process, because personnel changes within TCL meant a far more aggressive approach towards the relationship with TfL: 'Paul Davison came in to fix the position for TCL's funders – that was his strength and he was good at it. I would not doubt that for one minute. He had a job to do and from TCL's perspective he did about as good a job as you could ask anybody to do; he got TCL out of the contract.

'We had a good working relationship and at no time did we get to a position where our relationship was irretrievably bad – it was a challenging relationship

2543 is about to stop at East Croydon on 13 March 2007 with a Line 1 service to West Croydon.
(Photo: Gareth Prior)

2549 arrives at Wandle Park on 13 September 2007 with a Line 3 service to New Addington.
(Photo: Gareth Prior)

One of the now-removed ticket machines can be seen on the left at Sandilands on 12 March 2008, where 2532 on a service to West Croydon passes 2540 on another Line 1 service to Elmers End.
(Photo: Gareth Prior)

because clearly if you are dealing with a company that is teetering on the brink of bankruptcy, then it is always going to be a difficult relationship, because that company is having to make really difficult decisions on a daily basis.'

All was not plain sailing, however, in the legal action brought by TfL against TCL, with Judge Mr Justice Tomlinson ruling that certain contractual provisions relating to accommodation and future capacity enhancement were simply requirements in the original design of the system and not ongoing operational requirements.

Livingstone in the spotlight

Mayor Ken Livingstone was forced to defend TfL's action when asked by Conservative Greater London Assembly member Andrew Pelling if he agreed with the judge's comment that the action brought against TCL was 'absurd'.

In another typically robust outburst, Livingstone's 20 April 2016 response stated: 'Mr Justice Tomlinson did not rule that the action brought against Tramtrack Croydon Limited by TfL was absurd. The action sought to provide contractual certainty as to where responsibility lay for dealing with requirements to enhance capacity.

'What the judge considered absurd was a provision in the Concession Agreement that states that on any occasion when passenger density exceeded 5 passengers per square metre, TCL was obliged to provide and pay for a capacity enhancement of 33% of the whole system. This was never part of TfL's pleaded or pursued case. On leading counsel's advice, TfL are appealing against the judgment to the Court of Appeal on several issues, not least that the concessionaire ought to be obliged to contribute investment to enhance capacity with its own money.'

In a report to the TfL Board the following month (24 May 2006), Transport

2547 approaches Dundonald Road on 10 October 2008 with a Line 3 service to New Addington. (Photo: Gareth Prior)

Commissioner Peter Hendy updated members on the legal situation as follows: 'London Trams [TfL] sought clarification from the courts over the obligations within the Concession Agreement for managing demand on the Tramlink system and investing in capacity enhancements. TfL's interpretation of the concession was that, having accepted demand and revenue risk, the PFI Concessionaire was responsible for funding and implementing capacity enhancements within prescribed limits.

'The court disagreed and found for TCL, maintaining that investment in capacity to meet demand was a matter for the public sector. Having considered the judgement, the clarifications given by the judge and legal advice, London Trams has applied for leave to appeal. This case deals with fundamental matters of principle within the PFI concession and the way in which risk is allocated and managed. It is important therefore that London Trams ensures that a precise interpretation of the Concession is obtained.'

Livingstone raises the stakes

As the legal process rumbled on during 2006, by the start of the following year the knives were well and truly out, and on 23 January 2007 Mayor Ken Livingstone called for TCL to step down from its role as operator of Tramlink. In a press statement, Livingstone claimed that TCL was in breach of its Concession Agreement and called for the management of TCL to resign and to sack the entire management team. This followed TfL's 'discovery' that TCL had been issued with two Improvement Notices by Her Majesty's Railway Inspectorate (HMRI) which TfL claimed it was not informed about, in breach of the Concession Agreement.

These Improvement Notices were both issued on 2 October 2006 and related to derailments at Phipps Bridge on 21 October 2005 and 25 May 2006 (see chapter 8). Responding to Livingstone's latest outburst, TCL acknowledged that HMRI had indeed issued two Improvement

2545 nears Arena
on 13 March 2007
with a Line 1 service
to West Croydon.
(Photo: Gareth Prior)

2541 comes off the single line at Mitcham Junction on 10 October 2008 with a Line 3 service to New Addington. (Photo: Gareth Prior)

Notices in October 2006 and that various recommendations were made by Rail Accident Investigation Branch (RAIB) following the derailments at Phipps Bridge, and were being acted upon.

One of these Improvement Notices concerned the visibility of what are known as Points Position Indicators (PPIs), a visual control measure to assist tram drivers in identifying incorrectly set points on the track ahead of them. The design in use at the time had been approved by HMRI before system opening, but the RAIB recommended that these be modified across the whole system to display a different visual pattern and bring the design into line with developing UK practice. TCL's risk assessment supported this view, and it was while pursuing the practicability of implementing this change to the PPIs that the Improvement Notice was issued to record and monitor progress to completion.

The second Improvement Notice related to an RAIB recommendation regarding the various alarms received at Tramlink's Control Room, following which a joint review by TCL and its operating company undertook to sort the alarms by risk, with the elimination of unnecessary alarms. As with the PPI issue, HMRI had told TCL that the Improvement Notices had been designed to act as a means of actually tracking progress rather than as a form of reprimand. TCL declared that it was on target to achieve a required completion date of 30 April 2007 and that rather than contest the notices, as was its right, it would simply press ahead with the system upgrades.

TCL fights back

TCL Managing Director Paul Davison fought back by declaring, 'TfL has been aware of these matters since the initial RAIB report recommendations in March 2006. At the time we had been advised by HMRI that these notices had been issued

for monitoring purposes and to ensure the system was brought up to developing UK practice. As TfL was already aware of the issue we did not rush into print to inform them, but briefed relevant TfL staff in routine meetings held in November 2006. Other matters relating to track-work were discussed with all relevant parties, including TfL and HMRI, to confirm incorporation within TCL's regular track renewal programme.

'Whilst we would never seek to trivialise any matter connected with safety we do have to question TfL's sense of proportion, given the nature of the matters concerned,' continued Davison. 'The Mayor's press release indicated that TfL does not know the nature of the actions required by HMRI. As we have a contract with them we might have expected them to have made contact with us, voicing any concerns they may have in the first instance. The notices require TCL to take "reasonably practical measures" to address the issues. The TCL Board considered

the matter in November and the actions proposed. TCL therefore rejects any suggestion that the company is not a fit and proper concessionaire for the Croydon Tramlink.'

'This leaves me no choice but to call for the directors of Tramtrack Croydon Ltd to resign and for the company to sack its entire management team,' countered Mayor Livingstone. 'I would urge the banks and shareholders to hand the company over to Transport for London so it can be safely, efficiently and reliably managed, allowing those who live or work in Croydon to enjoy the service they deserve. There have only ever been three Improvement Notices issued in total to modern tramways in the UK. The fact that Tramtrack Croydon Ltd is the recipient of two of these Notices relating to the management of the network clearly shows the company is not fit to run a public transport system.'

Livingstone's move came a fortnight after a previous onslaught against TCL,

2540 pauses at Avenue Road on 12 March 2008 with a Line 2 service to Beckenham Junction. (Photo: Gareth Prior)

2540 stops at Arena on 10 October 2008 with a Line 2 service to Beckenham Junction, passing 2537 on a line 1 service to West Croydon.
(Photo: Gareth Prior)

2550 approaches Arena from Elmers End on 10 October 2008 with a Line 1 service to West Croydon.
(Photo: Gareth Prior)

criticising its maintenance record, and
blaming TCL for a failure to improve
Sunday services, despite demand.
Livingstone published four photographs of
road surface defects in Addiscombe Road
to support his claims, the most serious of
which was a pothole caused by a cross-
drain defect.

In response to this first press release,
TCL said it had repaired the drain, and
would have carried out the surfacing work
had Croydon Council allowed roadworks
in the run-up to Christmas. It added that
capacity problems on the New Addington
line were the result of TfL not providing
the 25th tram, which it had sought during
the arguments over opening the Centrale
tram stop, and concluded by saying that
TCL operates the service which is specified
by TfL.

A decisive legal defeat for TCL

Many months of legal wrangling came to
a conclusion on 31 January 2007, one week
after Mayor Livingstone's call for TCL to
forfeit its concession. What would finally
lead to an end of the PFI deal during the
following year was the loss by TCL of
the court case it had brought against the
TfL subsidiary London Bus Services Ltd,
seeking compensation on a cash fare basis
for new tickets and passes introduced on
the Tramlink network, which could have
amounted to over £6m per year at 2006
rates. While the vast majority of Tramlink
passengers used pre-paid tickets, such
as travelcards or Oyster pay-as-you-go,
which are cheaper than a single cash fare,
TfL had consistently made clear that TCL
was not entitled to the full cash fare value
for each journey made on Tramlink, as it
had claimed.

In an announcement entitled
'Tramtrack Croydon Ltd loses case for
cash fare compensation', TfL set out its
position by declaring: 'TfL looks to act
fairly and reasonably when negotiating
compensation levels, but have always
maintained Tramtrack Croydon Ltd
should receive compensation and not a

2532 arrives at
Dundonald Road on
10 October 2008
with a Line 3 service
to New Addington.
(Photo: Gareth Prior)

2550 approaches
Arena on 10 October
2008 with a
Line 2 service to
West Croydon.
(Photo: Gareth Prior)

2535 stands
at Centrale on
10 October 2008
with a Line 3 service
to New Addington.
(Photo: Gareth Prior)

subsidy. To that end, TfL has adopted a "no better, no worse" approach, in other words, although Tramtrack Croydon Ltd should be no worse off because of the introduction of new tickets or passes, neither should they be better off. This policy was the basis of a proposed new agreement TfL sought to reach with Tramtrack Croydon Ltd in 2003 in relation to compensation for new tickets and passes, but negotiations on that agreement stalled for almost two years because of this court case.'

Phil Hewitt, Head of London Trams, said: 'The court's ruling on this case is a complete vindication of Transport for London's policy for compensation on a "no better, no worse" basis. Tramtrack Croydon Ltd's claim for compensation on a cash fare basis would have constituted a windfall for the company, and we

do not believe the public purse should subsidise a private company in this way. The Judge's ruling has ringingly endorsed our approach. We hope that Tramtrack Croydon Ltd will think twice before launching any further misguided actions against Transport for London.

'The Mayor has recently voiced serious concerns about Tramtrack Croydon Ltd's ability to run a transport system; I sincerely hope that now this issue has been resolved, Tramtrack Croydon Ltd will focus their energies on running the Croydon Tramlink system and providing a safe, reliable service for passengers. We would welcome proposals from the company for their future revenue growth and for their investment in the infrastructure to ensure the network is in a state of good repair and keeps up with growing demand.'

TRAMS IN THE TOWN CENTRE

2530 departs East Croydon on 8 November 2018 for Elmers End.

2550 (New Addington) and 2542 (Wimbledon) at East Croydon on 5 April 2019.

2563 travels along the tram reservation in George Street on 5 April 2019.

2555 approaches East Croydon on 5 April 2019.

A view looking west on 5 April 2019 towards the George Street stop.

2558 pauses at Wellesley Road stop on 5 April 2019.

2558 makes its way onto Crown Hill on 5 April 2019.

2544 descends
Crown Hill on
8 November 2018.

2544 in Church
Street on
8 November 2018.

2549 in Church Street on 5 April 2019.

2558 at Church Street stop on 5 April 2019, where its destination display has just changed from West Croydon to New Addington.

2543 at Church Street stop on 5 April 2019 with a West Croydon.

CHAPTER 6

PROJECT SEAGULL AND TfL TAKEOVER

A trio of running themes characterised the eight years in which TCL ran Tramlink, and the conflict the consortium found itself in with TfL, which eventually led to its exit. First of these was the issue over fares, as outlined in the previous chapter. Inter-related to this was the issue of bus competition, where TCL maintained that TfL had not honoured the terms of the Concession Agreement and that, instead of removing competing bus routes, it had increased bus mileage in Croydon by 32% in the first five years of the Concession (2000–2005), with cash bus fares on competing routes 20% cheaper than the tram, until the January 2004 fares reforms, while day and season ticket holders were paying 30% less on buses than on the trams.

The third critical issue concerned increasing passenger capacity, which was already becoming an issue at peak times, even before the 2004 fares reforms. Under the terms of the Concession Agreement, the concessionaire was required to provide up to 33% additional capacity, but there was an argument over when that should be provided and who should pay for it. TfL's argument in court was that TCL had included plans for how it could go about extending the trams and modify the vehicles to provide the extra capacity, so TfL's expectation was that this was what TCL was going to do. Its response was that no, it was just indicative, and TCL had never undertaken to do the work.

In this argument there would be no winner or loser. From the TfL perspective, if it was found liable for providing the increased capacity, it would have to fund it, if and when it was needed. On the other hand, if TCL were found liable for the capacity, it would not have been able to fund it, so that would have been a trigger

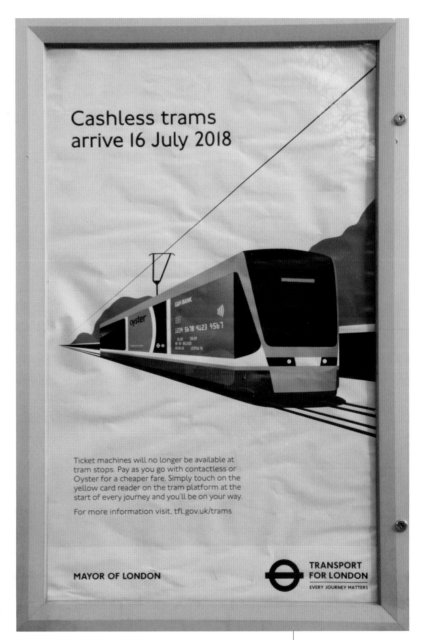

Cashless trams arrive 16 July 2018

Ticket machines will no longer be available at tram stops. Pay as you go with contactless or Oyster for a cheaper fare. Simply touch on the yellow card reader on the tram platform at the start of every journey and you'll be on your way.

For more information visit. tfl.gov.uk/trams

MAYOR OF LONDON

TRANSPORT FOR LONDON
EVERY JOURNEY MATTERS

A poster heralding the July 2018 end of cash fares on Tramlink.

for the consortium to say that it wanted out. In the event, the legal ruling was that TCL was required to prepare for additional capacity, but that there was no obligation at any point to specifically provide it, so effectively the judgment was hollow.

Taking the dispute to court

'We believed that we [TfL] should have been able to trigger that when crowding limits were breached and you got above four passengers per sq. metre, and that you [TCL] should then be investing in the infrastructure,' explains former TfL Head of Trams Phil Hewitt. 'But that was not a clear trigger, and it was decided that this sort of trigger had to be explicitly spelled out if you were going to rely on it. Broadly, both sides could have claimed

victory, but TCL's was the stronger, in that they really didn't have any obligation to do anything at any particular point in time.

'That clarity was what we were really after by going to court, because the outcome was going to be the same either way. It would either trigger a termination from TCL's perspective, saying it would not invest and so putting itself in breach of its concession, or we were going to have to fund it. Either way we were going to have to spend money, so that was the key bit of clarity we needed. We were in a position where we were going to have to fund the investment, and TCL was not going to get any more money, so both sides needed to come to the table.'

The dispute was quite technical, but there was a commercial rationale

Two generations of vehicle pass in Addiscombe Road on 28 January 2019, with 2560 bound for Elmers End as 2549 approaches with a West Croydon service.

behind it, so instead of invoking the dispute process set out in the Concession Agreement, the two parties (Paul Davison at TCL and Phil Hewitt at TfL) agreed that they would go straight to court and get a final decision. Once determined, the question then was how was TCL going to be able to walk away with its funders feeling that they had done the best they could, and how would TfL keep the system going and be able to invest in an economically viable way, that was not just handing over vast swathes of cash to the private sector?

Hewitt describes what became known as 'Project Seagull' as a challenging situation: 'Conclusion of the court cases really facilitated discussions about how the network could be taken forward. It came down to a straight financial transaction for TfL – when we looked at it, the bottom line was that the fares compensation formula was there and was still paying out. Looking at fares policy positions and where we were going, it was fairly easy to do the forward projections and work out that it would be cleaner and cheaper for us to buy the network rather than continue to pay out fares compensation, so it was a straight financial business case which said that TfL can save money by buying the TCL concession out.

'I ran some analysis as we got to the end of the negotiation which effectively said that we had paid across the ten years or so no more for Tramlink by putting it through the PFI route and buying it back than we would have paid if we had simply put all the money up front. The difference being that for the first twelve years of its life – from 1996 to 2008 – those risks had been taken by the private sector and the public sector had been insulated from them. So the bottom line was that from a public sector perspective, it looked like Croydon had been quite a good deal. We hadn't spent any more money than if we had paid cash for it, and we had been insulated from all of the construction risks and from all of the early operational risks.'

Negotiating a takeover

The Project Seagull negotiations went on for most of 2007 and into 2008, with the TfL team being led from an operational and engineering perspective by Phil Hewitt, alongside Finance Director Richard Webster and a TfL corporate finance team headed by Matthew Reagan. One way of achieving the takeover that was examined was termination of the 99-year PFI contact with TCL, which TfL had the option of terminating, but that would have meant un-picking all of the contracts supporting the concession. These were largely felt to be fit for purpose however, so the option chosen was for TfL to buy TCL and then for TfL to step into all of its existing contractual relationships.

Under the terms of the deal, the bank debt of TCL was purchased by TfL for £98m, and the company's equity was bought for a token £1.00, giving TfL ownership of TCL. Looking at how that figure was arrived at, the original PFI comprised a £125m grant from government and £80m put in by the private sector. There were also various claims which Amey McAlpine had against TCL on the books as well, and various changes to the debt profile had been put in place as part of TCL's earlier restructuring. What the deal meant however, was that TfL did not pay any more to acquire Tramlink than it would have done if it had simply put up £205m at the start of the project.

Formal news that TCL had accepted TfL's offer of £98m was announced on 17 March 2008, when Mayor Livingstone triumphantly declared: 'Bringing Tramlink into the control of TfL is excellent news for Londoners. This will mean we can plan how to make the improvements that are required to cater for ever increasing numbers of passengers and provide them with the very best possible services. It will allow us to build on the success of Tramlink to date, and increase levels of investment in the system to ensure it can keep up with growing demand, all the

A pleasantly rural scene near Lloyd Park on 28 January 2019, as 2536, bound for West Croydon, passes 2545 heading towards New Addington.

while providing a safe, reliable service for passengers.'

Justifying the price being paid, TfL's 17 March 2008 announcement said its current contract with TCL required TfL to make compensation payments for changes to the fares and ticketing policy introduced since 1996. In 2007 that payment was £4m, and the rate was increasing annually. Taking control of Tramtrack Croydon Ltd meant TfL would no longer have to make those payments and would be able to concentrate on improving the network. Peter Hendy, TfL Commissioner, added: 'With 88 years remaining on the Concession Agreement with Tramtrack Croydon Ltd, this deal represents excellent value for money for London's fare and tax payers.'

TfL takes control

Setting out its vision for Tramlink, TfL declared that there would be no change to

current fares and ticketing arrangements, but improvements already proposed would take effect as soon as TfL took control of the network. Off-peak services to Elmers End and Beckenham Junction would double from two trams per hour to four on Monday to Saturday evenings and on Sundays. TfL would also seek to run additional services to relieve crowding on the Wimbledon to New Addington line. In addition, graffiti and vandalism on the system would be targeted, general maintenance levels would increase, and TfL would begin a programme to refresh tram interiors and stops to improve the environment for passengers.

Speaking in rather blunter terms to the *Evening Standard* (11 April 2008) about the proposed TfL takeover, Mayor Livingstone said: 'The Croydon tram is vital to the hundreds of thousands of Londoners who use it, but has been allowed to gradually fall into disrepair. It is a reminder that the Conservative policy of privatising vital

transport services has failed. Long-term investment and even basic maintenance ground to a halt when the owner was not making enough profit to repay its debt. If I'm re-elected as Mayor [he wasn't] we will immediately get to work cleaning up stations, refurbishing trains and improving safety. And we will start upgrading trains and track, adding more capacity with extra carriages and extending the line to Crystal Palace.'

On 23 June 2008, TfL's London Rail Managing Director Ian Brown told *Rail Business Intelligence* magazine that although TfL had plans to extend the Tramlink network, his immediate concern was to tackle the maintenance backlog previously highlighted by Mayor Livingstone: 'The shelters, the trams are dowdy. We want to do the fabric stuff first before the grand stuff.' Brown added that TfL Commissioner Peter Hendy was 'very keen that the frequency is not less than every 15 minutes. Half-hourly for a tram network, especially in the evening, is not really trying very hard'.

Managing the change of ownership

As part of the takeover by TfL, Phil Hewitt's role changed in June 2008 from being TfL's Head of Trams, to Director, London Tramlink. Speaking a decade later in his Birmingham office, where he is now head of Midland Metro, Hewitt vividly recalls the issues and challenges which he and his team faced in taking over and running the Tramlink network:

'June 2008 was when we bought the shares [TCL], got the keys and stepped into those contractual relationships. It was very challenging because we had to put a team together of competent people, so we could assure the Railway Inspectorate and ORR that we were competent to fulfil our duties. We didn't have time to recruit people, there was not a lot of forward notice that a deal was capable of being done and what the likely outcome of that deal was going to be, it was a matter of a couple of months, so we brought in contract staff. That was always going to be a challenge, but we got through it.

2564 arrives at Arena on 6 November 2018 with a Beckenham Junction service.

A busy scene at the Chepstow Road crossing on 8 November 2018, where 2562 approaches with an Elmers End service as 2548/60 head west to West Croydon and Wimbledon respectively.

'None of the existing TCL management team transferred across on the takeover and that reflected the fact that relationships had got quite fractious, and relationships between people above me and TCL were particularly poor. There was a fair degree of ill-feeling and things had been said by people which should just never have been said. It was not a happy ship, and the problem also was that the relationship between TCL and FirstGroup had fractured as well. Indeed there was an RAIB report which criticised TCL relating to a derailment, which essentially said that the contract had become a blocker to effective management of the network.

'That's not a good thing to have written, so we realised that the only way we were going to change relationships was to change some of the key personnel. That meant we had to put a shadow team in place to be ready to step in and run Tramlink as

the concessionaire. The main thing was that the operator (FirstGroup) carried on doing the operator's job, Carillion carried on maintaining the infrastructure and Bombardier were maintaining the trams. So the key suppliers were unaffected. TCL was effectively a holding company – the Carillion contract was managed through TCL for example, so when we took over TCL those contractual relationships stayed.

'Where we could we used the existing TfL Trams team to provide some support as well. A lot of the technical support was brought in from Interfleet Technology [a consultancy firm] – all key people with light railway experience. We also moved the tram business in TfL from surface transport into London Rail, which seemed a better fit – under Ian Brown and Howard Smith – so it sat alongside DLR and London Overground. That was specifically from a safety regulations perspective, because it seemed rather odd to have one rail business sitting

within surface transport and all the other rail businesses in another part of the organisation.'

Another perspective on the takeover

Perhaps not surprisingly, one of the senior figures within Tramtrack Croydon Limited remembers the build-up to takeover in 2007 and early 2008 rather differently from Phil Hewitt. Jim Snowdon was Engineering Manager at TCL and one of only two individuals (the other being Charles Tomlinson, Head of Safety) who had been with the consortium for the whole eleven years since the Concession Agreement had been signed in 1996. His role was effectively that of Chief Engineer and was number two in the line of responsibility if anything went wrong.

Snowdon recalls the slow and painful build-up to the TfL takeover: 'It was fairly acrimonious, because in 2006/7 we had a string of consultants and others brought in by TfL to try and find fault with what we were doing. There was a clause in the contract that allowed TfL to take over if it was deemed that TCL was not fit to run the tramway. So they did quite a lot of that, and people like myself spent quite a lot of time saying "No, what you are saying is rubbish."

'Eventually TfL relented and started to talk about commercial offers, and that was at a stage when TCL was getting a bit schizophrenic. I can remember in 2007 we were actually looking at the practicalities of getting some additional trams and other upgrades to the system, which would have required investment, yet at the same time TCL management was busy negotiating with the banks and with TfL towards the takeover.

'We as staff got a warning – we went through the charade of what is called "job mapping" – looking out how closely our existing jobs would map across into what TfL thought the new structure would be and then, with no surprise, we found we were deemed redundant. So, with the exception of

A single car pursues 2552 as it heads along Addiscombe Road towards the Lebanon Road stop on 6 November 2018 with a New Addington service.

the office secretary we, as the knowledgeable people in TCL, were just dumped.'

On the Monday of the TfL takeover, the secretly-assembled shadow management team from Interfleet took over the management of Tramlink. Snowdon was quietly poached by the consultancy firm, because it thought his experience might be useful, put in a light rail job, but never again allowed anywhere near Croydon: 'One day I had said I would like to go there and have a look at some of the track renewal that was being done, work I had instigated, but which TfL was now doing,' he remembers. 'I was dropped a very big hint that I would not be going. I may have been the person who knew too much.'

Improvements and challenges for the new team

Tramlink's new owners wasted no time in delivering on the promised improvements. Only a month after

completing the takeover (in June 2008) came an announcement on 14 July 2008 of imminent changes: 'In the first of a series of improvements to the Croydon Tramlink, from 20 July TfL will increase the tram service on the Beckenham Junction and Elmers End routes so that trams run every 15 minutes during evenings and Sundays. This improvement will make travel more convenient for passengers and brings the tram timetable into line with the TfL policy of providing a 'turn up and go' service.'

Newly-elected London Mayor, Boris Johnson, commented: 'One of the major reasons for Transport for London taking control of the Croydon Tramlink last month was to improve the service for the passengers who rely on it. Passengers have told us that they need a more frequent service, and I'm pleased that we have been able to deliver this so swiftly. This is the first of many improvements that will be designed to make Tramlink, and the rest of the transport network, more convenient, reliable and safe.'

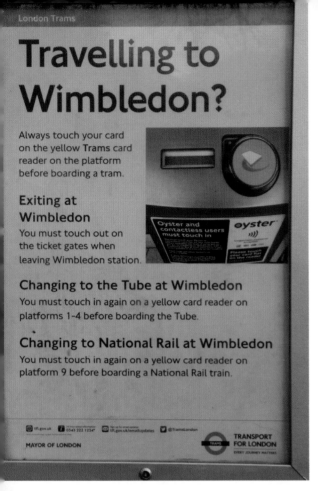

Travelling to Wimbledon?

Always touch your card on the yellow **Trams** card reader on the platform before boarding a tram.

Exiting at Wimbledon

You must touch out on the ticket gates when leaving Wimbledon station.

Changing to the Tube at Wimbledon

You must touch in again on a yellow card reader on platforms 1-4 before boarding the Tube.

Changing to National Rail at Wimbledon

You must touch in again on a yellow card reader on platform 9 before boarding a National Rail train.

MAYOR OF LONDON   TRANSPORT FOR LONDON EVERY JOURNEY MATTERS

Passengers using Wimbledon station are reminded about the need for 'touching in' on the correct card reader.

London Trams are cashless and paper tickets are no longer available here. For more information visit tfl.gov.uk/ways-to-pay

Ticket machines at stops were shrouded in covers after the ending of cash fares in July 2018 and before their eventual removal.

Managing Director of TfL London Rail, Ian Brown, added: 'We are pleased to be able to reduce waiting times so soon after taking over Tramlink. These apparently small improvements will make a big difference for our passengers. We are also working on a number of other upgrades, including refurbishing trams and stops and improving policing on the network.'

Within two months of TfL's taking ownership of Tramlink, Hewitt and his team faced their first real challenge. He recalls Tramlink as being 'a lucky system and nothing much had gone wrong for several years'. But in September 2008 there were two fatal incidents in a week, which put a huge strain on the new team. One was a bus crashing into a tram (7 September 2008) and the other was a cyclist hit by a tram (Morden Hall, 13 September 2008 and detailed in Chapter 8), which led to a Rail Accident Investigation Branch report and the issue by the RAIB of an Improvement Notice.

'This led to some changes in how the network was managed, because we found that changes had been made to the network that no-one was aware of, and footways had been modified – it was quite sobering to get to that position,' recalls Hewitt. 'It led to improvements which were cascaded upwards and nationally as well as a result, so although they were terrible events you can learn from them and do things better. But they put a lot of strain on the incoming management team.'

Extensive track renewals

As if dealing with the two fatal incidents was not enough, Hewitt and his new team were also faced with addressing the infrastructure issues which outgoing London Mayor Ken Livingstone had slammed when he said Tramlink had been allowed to 'gradually fall into disrepair' by its private sector owners:

'The biggest challenge we faced really was that the Croydon town centre track work was in a pretty sorry state,' explains Hewitt. 'At East Croydon all the switches and crossings were pretty much life-expired. The curve at Barclays Bank on George Street East was also life-expired, although it had already been replaced once before. There were some problems with the infrastructure where it had been built over the Wellesley Road underpass, and then there was the track down at Reeves Corner, that was pretty much shot as well.

2530 follows the former railway line south of Addiscombe as it approaches the sharp right-hand bend at Sandilands on 8 November 2018 with a Wimbledon-bound service.

'So there was quite an extensive programme of track replacement work needed early on that required closure of the Croydon loop for several weeks. This was a huge undertaking and was when we introduced a temporary tram stop called Dingwall Road – a single platform temporary stop that we built to terminate trams coming in from Wimbledon while East Croydon was dug up and we could not access it. That was good and quite innovative.

'We were running a split service at the time, which meant that trams were being out-stabled on the far side of the network in the tunnels at Sandilands. This was for about six weeks during the school summer holidays – it was a big undertaking and we remodelled East Croydon at the same time, because some of the switches [points] were in places where they were getting damaged by crossing traffic, so we took the opportunity to do quite a bit of relaying work.'

A new look and new trams

Besides embarking on the extensive track replacement programme, another very visible change to be made by the new team came in October 2008 and was a refresh of the tram stops and the introduction of a new livery. Out went the traditional red and in came the green livery that is in use today, a means of distinguishing trams from the local buses, and the system's brand name was changed from Croydon Tramlink to London Tramlink, a mark of longer term ambitions to expand the network.

Addressing the issue of service pattern and frequency, changes that came in with the enhanced frequencies to Beckenham Junction and Elmers End, mentioned above, included running additional services on the Wimbledon branch as far as Therapia Lane, and using the depot there as a turn-back facility. The early months of TfL ownership also saw a restructuring of services to New Addington and, coming at

Another rural scene, this time between Fieldway and Addington Village, with 2552 bound for West Croydon on 8 November 2018.

a time when one vehicle (2534) was out of service for an extended period following the George Street crash of 7 September 2008, it became clear to the new team that there was not a lot of resilience in the fleet, with some timetable cuts having to be made in order to maintain a reliable service.

'The need for more trams emerged in 2010 as something we wanted to do, so 18 months after the takeover we had a plan and looked at whether there were trams we could get from elsewhere in Europe,' explains Phil Hewitt. 'There were some vehicles similar to the CR4000 trams [the existing fleet] running in Utrecht, which were the same basic design and we did look at whether we could take six of them on, but that didn't work.

'We also looked at whether or not we could procure trams from Edinburgh. We would have modified them and taken a couple of suspended sections out to fit them on the platforms, and that looked like it ought to be a bit of a win-win for

us and for Edinburgh, because we needed trams and Edinburgh had too many trams, so you would have thought that would be an easy win. But we couldn't get a credible and commercial deal so it was more economical and less risky for us to buy new.'

While Tramlink services had remained relatively static (between 2.4 and 2.7 million km per annum) since 2000, what was driving the need for more capacity was a 45% increase in annual passenger journeys during the first ten years of the system, with the 18.6 million journeys made in 2001/02 forecast to have increased to 27.8 million by the end of 2010/11.

Procuring new trams

In January 2011, the now TfL-owned TCL opened a tender for the supply of ten new or second-hand trams for use between Therapia Lane and Elmers End. That was followed on 1 March 2011 by an announcement from TfL entitled 'New trams to help boost Croydon's economy a step closer' which confirmed that Croydon Council's Finance Committee had ratified a £3m contribution towards the deal, a move that was applauded by London Mayor, Boris Johnson, and Croydon Council Leader, Mike Fisher.

Commenting on his Council's financial support, Fisher said: 'Croydon's trams are an icon of the borough's vision and ambition. Getting more trams on the system as soon as possible is the answer to pressing capacity issues as the popularity of Tramlink continues to grow.' Giving his endorsement, Boris Johnson added: 'This is a great example of teamwork between two authorities to provide investment that will improve services for outer Londoners. The new trams will be a real win for local

people living or working in Croydon, Wimbledon, Beckenham and New Addington.'

Under EU regulations, the Europe-wide invitation to tender for the additional trams had been published in the *Official Journal of the European Union*, with bids closing at midday on 14 March 2011. Following this, pre-qualified bidders would be announced, and then a supplier appointed and a contract let. Delivery was to be by summer 2011 and the competition was open for either new build trams, or second-hand vehicles that could be modified at reasonable cost to run on the London Tramlink infrastructure.

On 24 March 2011 London Mayor Boris Johnson was able to announce that three parties had been shortlisted for the supply contract and that the three bidders, City of

Despite being close to Central Croydon, a delightful lack of traffic in Addiscombe Road is evident on 28 January 2019 as 2536 heads for New Addington.

Edinburgh/CAF, Stadler (Stadler Pankow GmBH) and Pesa (Pojazdy Szynowe PESA Bydgoszcz S.A. Holding) would now be invited to submit proposals to supply the additional trams, which would increase the frequency of services on the busiest parts of the network between Therapia Lane, central Croydon and Elmers End. Showing some slippage from previous aspirations, this announcement talked about delivery of the new vehicles during the latter part of 2011, for a possible start of service in early 2012

Paying a visit to inspect one of the existing trams at East Croydon tram stop, Johnson commented: 'I have no greater responsibility as Mayor than to ensure people can move around this city with ease, comfort and reliability. Trams in Croydon have proved a major success and this is reflected in journey numbers which have soared by 45% since the network opened in 2000. I look forward to the extra vehicles developing this vital, much-appreciated, and indeed attractive, form of transport further.'

A further enhancement to services came shortly after the tender short-list announcement when, on 31 May 2011, increased weekday evening services were introduced on the Wimbledon to New Addington route, which covered more than half the tram network. From that date, the existing eight-trams-an-hour service that operated between 07:00 and 19:00 was extended until 21:00, after which it would reduce to four trams per hour. 'We are pleased to be able to offer passengers an increase in this service, which will make off-peak evening travel more appealing and convenient, with trams running every seven to eight minutes,' declared Director of Tramlink, Phil Hewitt, 'It is part of TfL's ongoing campaign to make tram travel a more popular option for travellers.'

Violence and the aftermath

Early August 2011 saw Croydon suffer from an unprecedented wave of violence and rioting that had spread across London to many other parts of the country, following the police shooting in Tottenham

2538 approaches Oaks Road Level Crossing, between Lloyd Park and Coombe Lane, on 28 January 2019 with a service for New Addington.

2548 runs alongside the railway line serving West Croydon and is about to ascend onto the Wandle Park flyover on 28 January 2019, with a Wimbledon service.

on 4 August of Mark Duggan, a 29-year-old father of four. On Monday, 8 August, the worst night of violence, a 26-year-old man from Brixton, Trevor Ellis, died in a shooting in Croydon and in one of the most disturbingly memorable images from that night, the landmark Reeves Furniture store in the town centre, a building and business dating from 1867 that had withstood two world wars, was destroyed in an arson attack, bringing Tramlink services to a temporary halt.

Having paid another visit to Croydon later that week, Mayor Boris Johnson linked his appreciation with how the disruption had been handled with an announcement on 18 August that contracts had been signed for six new trams. They would provide a boost to services from early 2012, and contribute to the regeneration of Croydon following the disturbances. At the same time local people were reminded that there would be free travel on the trams during the coming weekend (20/21 August 2011), which it

was hoped would encourage shoppers to head into the town centre and support their local businesses.

'I was deeply moved by my visits to Croydon last week and I was greatly heartened by the determination of local people not to let the mindless behaviour of a few members of our society leave a permanent mark on this community,' declared Johnson. 'Our Tramlink team did a great job of restoring tram services to the town centre so rapidly following the disturbances, and we hope the signing of contracts for the six new trams will provide a real boost to services when they begin running early next year.'

Six brand new trams were being supplied under a £16.3m contract, which included spare parts and special equipment to run the vehicles. These were to be built by Swiss manufacturer Stadler and were known as its 'Variobahn' model, based on vehicles currently in use in Bergen, Norway. At 33 metres long, the Stadler trams would be 2.5 metres

longer than the existing fleet, were air-conditioned, and low-floor, giving better accessibility.

The first of the new trams was to be delivered in winter 2011, entering service in spring 2012 following a rigorous testing and commissioning period. The remaining five trams would then arrive from early 2012 through to spring 2012. Each Variobahn tram comprised five sections, with wide gangways between each giving them a more spacious interior. To accommodate them and the planned additional services, modifications would be required to extend tram stops and increase depot capacity at Therapia Lane.

Linking the tram order to recent troubles, Croydon Council Leader Mike Fisher said: 'Perception is important – and the perception today is that things are really beginning to move again in Croydon; and by spending heavily on extra trams we're backing what we're saying with hard cash. The tram network has proved to be a huge hit with the many thousands who use it on a daily basis.

It's fair to say that, at peak times during the day, the network has become a victim of its success. These new trams will ease that burden, providing an even better service for the network's customers and help ensure its continued success into the future.'

Just a month after the disturbances in Croydon, the area and transport system were not only back on their feet, but described by TfL as 'fighting fit' – with Tramlink recording its busiest day during normal transport operation. On 23 September 2011 a total of 102,000 passengers boarded trams, a record breaking figure that marked an almost 20% increase on the average daily (weekday) passenger count during 2011 of 87,000.

Winning an award

Such was the Tramlink team's success at restoring normal services following the disturbances that, on 5 October 2011, Tramlink won a Special Award for

The tram reservation alongside George Street in Central Croydon, seen on 28 January 2019 as 2565 approaches East Croydon station bound for Beckenham Junction while 2532 heads towards Wimbledon.

Outstanding Achievement at the National Light Rail Awards. The prize was given, 'in recognition of the dedication and effort of the London Tramlink recovery team in response to the disruption caused by the civil disturbances in August. London Tramlink worked quickly and effectively to restore a full service on the tram network, just two days after looters and arsonists had caused extensive damage to the tracks and cabling on which the tram network relies.'

Outlining why Tramlink had won the award, Howard Johnston, Publisher of *Tramways and Urban Transit* magazine and one of the judges, said: 'Within just 48 hours, the clearly well organised Tramlink team had re-erected the overhead lines,

made safe the damaged masts, cleared the clogged tracks, isolated the melted signals and had services back up and running under immensely difficult circumstances. This is a truly remarkable achievement and a worthy winner in this category.'

Safety improvements

Besides its work to improve frequencies and buy additional trams, another focus for TfL was to increase the safety of Tramlink. On 21 December 2011 came an announcement of measures including new road markings, improved visibility, enforcement by Tramlink officers and a publicity campaign aimed at making

2544 heads down Crown Hill and into Church Street on 8 November 2018 with a Wimbledon-bound service.

Tramlink's trams safer for passengers and other road users. It followed a period of 18 months in which there had been 46 incidents involving trams, the great majority of them relatively minor, such as wing mirrors being knocked off illegally parked cars. Major medical treatment was required in only two incidents and there was one fatality.

'Our tram system is very safe and drivers are trained to a high standard, but one accident is one too many and we will continue to work with everyone involved to reduce the potential for them to happen,' said Howard Smith, Chief Operating Officer for TfL London Rail. A public information campaign was launched using brightly-coloured images of bunches of flowers painted on the ground at fifteen spots in Croydon town centre where the tram tracks shared the same road space with cars and walkers. The campaign message, along with the flowers, was featured on posters throughout the tram network with the words 'Don't be remembered like this – watch out for trams'.

Other measures being taken to improve safety included the appointment of a team of six Tramlink neighbourhood officers working on the network to reassure passengers and prevent anti-social behaviour; installation of transparent panels, and vegetation maintenance work, to improve sightlines for drivers to ensure they could see pedestrians and that pedestrians could see approaching trams; and the repainting of road markings to show the 'swept path' of the trams more boldly. In addition, every foot crossing was reassessed and TfL was working closely with Croydon Council to find ways to make tram/pedestrian crossings even safer and with safety authorities to update the regulations on tram crossings and identify best practice.

A major milestone in work to upgrade Tramlink's infrastructure saw a six-day closure of the Croydon loop from 11-16 February 2012, as 200 metres of track in Crown Hill was replaced as part of Tramlink's Investment Programme, to give a much smoother ride than before. Commenting on the closure, Interim Director of London Tramlink Sharon Thompson said: 'This is necessary maintenance and upgrade work which needs to be done as it means a more reliable service for passengers as well as less wear and tear on our trams. We will keep inconvenience to passengers and businesses along the route to a minimum and complete the works as quickly as possible.'

Another enhancement offering benefit to Tramlink users, which was undertaken in early 2012, was the creation of a new entrance to West Croydon rail station, giving easier interchange and a more direct walking route between trains and the nearby tram stop and bus station. A wider gate in the new gate-line would allow customers who used wheelchairs, or travelled with a guide dog, buggy or large luggage, to use the entrance, which offered step-free access to Platform 4 on the station, without staff assistance.

New trams enter service

The long-awaited new trams, and additional service from Elmers End to Therapia Lane, became a reality on 25 June 2012, when Mayor Boris Johnson was able to announce that all six of the new Stadler trams were now in service, the first having been rolled out in February. This new service would bring the number of trams running each hour between Therapia Lane and Croydon town centre up from eight to twelve at peak times, by running four trams per hour between Therapia Lane and Elmers End. When on board, passengers would find the new trams trams were air conditioned, more spacious and equipped with better accessibility and safety features than the existing fleet, while their introduction also created twenty new jobs at London Tramlink.

Croydon Council leader Mike Fisher hailed the new trams, saying: 'These

2538 approaches Lloyd Park on 28 January 2019 with a service for West Croydon.

fantastic new trams are a major boost for a transport network that is the envy of London and the rest of the country and they will provide an even better service for people who live and work here. We have invested £3m into this project to help boost local infrastructure – and it's further evidence of our commitment to the regeneration of our borough. This year promises to be the beginning of an exciting period of delivery that will transform the way our town looks and operates.'

The six new trams would enable a direct service between Therapia Lane and Elmers End, where passengers currently had to change to make this journey, and increase the peak-time service at Elmers End from six trams per hour to eight. Acquisition of the new tram fleet formed part of a £23m Mayoral funding package designed help return Croydon to its former glory following the damage to its town centre in the August 2011 disturbances. In addition to the new trams, reliability

improvements to the Wimbledon branch were also anticipated by the end of 2012, with creation of a second track between Mitcham and Mitcham Junction removing a bottleneck in the system, and facilitating future work to increase frequency on the line to Wimbledon.

Further new vehicles ordered

That promise of improved frequency on the Wimbledon branch came a step closer just over one year on from the new route launch when, on 30 August 2013, came an announcement that Tramlink had ordered four further new trams, to deliver a 50% increase in capacity on the Wimbledon branch by 2016, the busiest route on the network. A £10.2m contract for the four new vehicles was under the terms of an option in the previous order for the six new trams delivered in 2012, with the first of these new vehicles being delivered during summer 2015 and the last scheduled to arrive in 2016.

The four additional Stadler trams (the order was later increased to six new vehicles) formed part of a much larger £30m Wimbledon Line Enhancement Programme and would complement the replacement of the single line sections between Mitcham and Mitcham Junction and between Mitcham Junction and Beddington Lane with double track, and the creation of an additional tram platform at Wimbledon station.

What was driving this ever-increasing need for additional capacity was the system's growing popularity, with ridership having hit a new record of 30.2 million passengers in 2012/3, up from 18.2 million in the first full year of operation. Forecasts suggested that population and employment growth would mean that by 2031 there would be a further 35% increase to 38.8 million passengers. 'This increase from eight to 12 trams per hour, with a 50% rise in capacity on the Wimbledon branch, will greatly improve tram frequency, reduce waiting times and increase reliability as well as making for a better passenger experience,' said TfL's Director of London Rail, Jonathan Fox.

Following improvements to accessibility at West Croydon railway station, another nearby development that would be of benefit to Tramlink users was a £4.5m upgrade of West Croydon Bus Station, first announced on 25 February 2014 and

No other road traffic is in evidence as Bombardier trams 2544 and 2541 pass in Addiscombe Road on 6 November 2018.

completed two years later, in early 2016. The bus station had been built in 1983 and was being used by 150 buses every hour, handling eight million passengers a year and being a popular interchange with both Tramlink and rail services. A total redesign would improve access for buses; provide improved facilities including fully accessible bus stops and CCTV coverage, as well as being designed to cope with a 20% increase in passenger numbers.

Improving Sunday service frequencies

A further enhancement of services on the Wimbledon branch came on Sunday, 14 December 2014, when the Sunday day-time (10.00–18.00hrs) frequency of trams running between Wimbledon and New Addington (Line 3) was doubled from one tram every fifteen minutes to one every seven to eight minutes. 'We're pleased to be able to bring these extra services into operation at a time of year when we know it is important for our passengers to have access to weekend shopping destinations,' commented TfL Director of London Tramlink Sharon Thompson. One month after the extra services were introduced the number of passengers using the line on Sundays had already risen by almost 10% from an average of 39,834 to 44,330.

At the same time that it announced the improved Sunday service (12 December 2014), TfL also confirmed that a new 700-metre section of double track had recently been completed between Mitcham Junction and Beddington Lane as part of the Wimbledon Line Enhancement Programme. Work was also in progress to add a new bay to Platform 10 at Wimbledon station, which would enable introduction of the additional four new trams onto the network, bringing a 50% increase for the Wimbledon branch and double the line's capacity in 2016.

Work to add the much-needed new bay to Platform 10 at Wimbledon station saw Wimbledon tram stop closed for more than three months from 13 July 2015, with services terminating at nearby Dundonald Road. This stop is a ten-minute walk from Wimbledon station and a signposted walking route was provided during closure, with tram tickets being accepted on local buses that connected Wimbledon with London's tram network. Completion of the work, and reopening of Wimbledon to trams, was announced on 2 November 2015, enabling a further four trams an hour to serve the stop from Spring 2016, when the new trams were due to enter service, allowing twelve trams an hour to serve Wimbledon.

That promised increase in service frequencies on the Wimbledon branch was duly delivered on Monday, 4 April 2016, when services between Wimbledon and Croydon increased from eight to twelve trams per hour. 'The Tram network is a crucial transport link to the community it serves and we are committed to continually improving our services. The extra trams will help meet increasing passenger demand and make a real difference to the customers who use the service every day,' commented Rory O'Neill, TfL's Director of Trams.

Two initiatives announced in spring 2016 were aimed at making life easier for Tramlink users. Firstly, live service information was made available for the first time, giving customers up-to-the-minute information about when their service would arrive and its destination, along with the status of the service, both through TfL's website and on Electronic Service Update Boards across other parts of the TfL network. Secondly, on 3 June 2016, Tramlink was added to TfL's tube map, a move designed to make it easier for those travelling to Wimbledon, Croydon or Beckenham to plan their journeys.

Early 2017 saw another line closure for upgrade work, when tram services were halted between Wimbledon and Mitcham from 11-20 February 2017 for a project to replace 750 metres of track between Morden Road and Merton Park, as well as replacing track and signals in the Dundonald Road crossing area. During

this period customers were advised to use a replacement bus service, serving Wimbledon, Morden Road and Mitcham tram stops, or use alternative local buses.

'Replacing the track and signals will reduce the need for further maintenance at these locations for many years to come and minimise future disruption for customers and local residents,' said Rory O'Neill, TfL's Director of Trams. 'In order to carry out our work safely and to keep the overall period of disruption to an absolute minimum, we need to close the tram service between Wimbledon and Mitcham for the duration of the works.'

Tramlink goes cashless

The first steps towards making Tramlink a cashless system were taken on 4 September 2017, when TfL began an eight-week public consultation on plans to remove ticket machines from tram stops and require all users to pay their fares with Oyster or contactless cards. Its argument was that the machines were only selling a small number of the more expensive paper tickets every week and did not allow customers to top up their Oyster cards. As the ticket machines, which were installed when the tram system opened in 2000, had such low usage and had reached the end of their useful life, it was no longer cost effective to maintain them or have them replaced.

In its public consultation, TfL noted that only 0.3% of single tram journeys were paid for with a ticket bought from a tram stop ticket machine, representing fewer than 250 tickets per day, with more than half of these sold from ten tram stops. A paper ticket bought from a ticket machine cost £2.60, whereas the equivalent pay-as-you-go single fare with Oyster or a contactless bank card was £1.50. Customers using pay-as-you-go also had access to the 'Hopper' fare, which gave a second tram or bus journey for free within one hour of touching in on the first tram or bus journey.

2543 pauses at Church Street on 31 October 2018 with a New Addington service.

2530 crosses the junction of Cherry Orchard Road just beyond East Croydon station on 6 November 2018 with a service for Elmers End.

Nine months after that consultation exercise was launched, TfL confirmed on 4 June 2018 that the ticket machines would be removed and the system would go cashless on 16 July 2018. This followed responses from more than 800 people to the consultation and came four years after London buses had gone cashless in July 2014. Since the proposal had been first announced, use of the existing ticket machines had fallen to the issue of just 66 single tickets a day, which meant that providing and maintaining ticket machines at every tram stop was not covered by ticket sales.

Having announced its decision to go cashless, TfL then began the formal process to allow for the machines to be removed and launched a marketing campaign across the network to ensure customers were aware of the changes before they were introduced. New signage was provided at tram stops to advise passengers on ways to pay, including how to download the TfL app and where to find their nearest Oyster Ticket Stop, with additional card validators installed at selected tram stops across the network to make it more convenient and quicker for passengers to touch in.

Commenting on the decision to go cashless, Mark Davis, General Manager of London Trams, said: 'The vast majority of tram customers already use pay-as-you-go with Oyster or contactless to travel, which is both cheaper than paper tickets and allows customers to use the Mayor's Hopper fare to make unlimited bus or tram journeys within an hour for £1.50. As very few ticket sales are made using ticket machines, we will be removing the existing cash ticket machines and encouraging customers to switch to pay-as-you-go, Travelcards or Bus & Tram Passes, all of which can quickly be bought from their local Oyster Ticket Stop, online or via the TfL app.'

A major timetable shake-up

In a move aimed at providing a more regular and reliable service to reduce passenger crowding a new timetable was introduced on 25 February 2018. In place of the existing four routes (1: Elmers End–West Croydon; 2: Beckenham Junction–West Croydon; 3: New Addington–Wimbledon; 4: Elmers End–Wimbledon), a revised service pattern meant that all but the first two trams of the day from New Addington would only run to West Croydon. This meant that the one in thirty passengers who wanted to make a

through journey would have to change in central Croydon.

The new service pattern saw services from Wimbledon running every five minutes to Central Croydon, with trams then running alternately on to Beckenham Junction or Elmers End, to give each of these destinations a ten-minute daytime frequency. New Addington services now operated every 7-8 minutes, although it remained a long-term TfL aspiration to increase the frequency on this route. In addition to these changes, extra early morning services to New Addington were introduced, extra evening services to both Beckenham Junction and Elmers End, and extra services both early morning and in the evening to Wimbledon.

TfL claimed the new timetable was designed to achieve a more even spacing of services throughout the day, removing long waits between trams, followed by several arriving at once, which could lead to overcrowding and difficulties in restoring services following delays. Rory O'Neill, TfL's General Manager of London Trams, commented: 'We have discussed these changes extensively with our customers and concluded that the new timetable will benefit the vast majority of tram users, ensuring services are more regular and less crowded.'

As part of this shake-up the familiar route numbers would no longer be displayed on the trams – a change which had already started with all Bombardier vehicles only displaying destinations – allowing a larger and clearer final destination to be shown on the trams for ease of use by passengers. What was also interesting to note from a number of visits paid to Tramlink in October and

2548 awaits attention on 16 January 2019 inside a spotlessly clean Therapia Lane depot.

November 2018 was that New Addington services were being entirely operated by the older Bombardier trams, with all the newer Stadler vehicles operating between Wimbledon and Beckenham Junction/ Elmers End.

Work on track upgrading saw yet another section of Tramlink closed in late March/early April 2018, as track was replaced between George Street and Church Street in central Croydon from 30 March until 4 April, and from the junction of Cherry Orchard Road to Addiscombe Road from 30 March until 8 April. This work formed part of a wider programme of routine track replacement on the network, which had seen the area of George Street from Wellesley Road to the High Street completed in 2017.

Tramlink today

Current Tramlink operations require 30 of the 35-strong fleet (2551 being out of service following the 2016 Sandilands disaster) to be in service every day, with the remaining five vehicles stabled or undergoing routine maintenance at the Therapia Lane depot. Based at the depot, Tram Operations Ltd has an operating department of some 20 people, comprising an operations manager, duty managers and control room staff. In addition to these, there are approximately 150 drivers and a 16-strong revenue protection team.

This team's role is principally the checking of tickets and processing of penalty fares, but they also play another important role, which is incident response. So in the case of a failed tram, the control room will attempt to organise its movement back to the depot, but if it is blocking a line and causing service disruption, or there is a sick person on a tram or a road traffic accident, the revenue protection team would go and assist in responding to the incident.

Tramlink is a hybrid between bus and rail operations and control room intervention would typically be similar to bus supervision, in that the signalling is all highway signalling. From the tram driver's point of view it will not give you a phase (line clear signal) until the vehicle is at the signal, and the driver will then just await the line clear signal to proceed. The control room is not generally a signalling operator, but is there to ensure that trams are correctly spaced out and to pass on information to customers by updating the Passenger Information Display screens at tram stops.

When an incident occurs the control room team will act like a bus controller would in handling the situation to minimise disruption. If a tram arrives at a stop and a passenger is ill and needs an ambulance, for example, the normal passage of trams would be interrupted, the system would then move into the railway world, where you have to control the movement of each individual tram, so it does not conflict with any other.

While the signalling will not allow bi-directional use of loops in platforms, there are a number of emergency operational procedures that drivers can implement to minimise any disruption when the system is in what is known as 'degraded operation'. At loops, where the points are normally sprung rather than motorised, drivers carry a bar that enables them to move the points manually in an emergency, to get round any obstruction such as a failed or halted tram.

Unlike many bus operators, Tramlink has no difficulty in recruiting and retaining its drivers. Some recruits come from the bus industry, because they are used to the shift patterns and for driving long periods in a day, but many come from other backgrounds. Once recruited, they undergo a training period of around twelve weeks, the exact duration being determined by track access, as any tuition on the network needs to be out of the way of the regular service, so not in peak periods and ideally off-peak or at night.

For recruits – who only need a current UK driving licence – there is a lot of classroom work, then they start by driving

in the depot sidings, before going onto a section of segregated track, and finally into traffic in central Croydon. By contrast to their train driving counterparts, Tramlink drivers get their route knowledge by default. With a system that is only 17½-miles long, a driver is likely to pass each location 3,000 times in a year, and a driver's roster would quite often cover the whole system in one day.

The popularity of Tramlink as a place to work is reflected in the very low level of staff turnover and the huge number of people wanting to become tram drivers. Despite occasional incidents, the level of customer satisfaction is high. Complaints on Tramlink are the lowest of any TfL transport mode, with customers generally liking and feeling reassured by trams as friendly, efficient and reliable.

2555 is the only tram present in the extensive sidings at Therapia Lane on 16 January 2019 as a Bombardier vehicle passes on a Wimbledon line service.

CHAPTER 7

A TOUR OF THE NETWORK

Wimbledon–Croydon

Our tour of the Tramlink network begins on Platform 10 of Wimbledon station, a hugely important interchange with both South Western Railway and Thameslink suburban services and London Underground's District Line. Since the 2015/6 upgrade work, this platform has been split in two, with a spur off the single running line serving newly created Platform 10b, where the platform face has been extended eastwards and means one tram can leave the station moments after another has arrived.

The track layout here is severely constrained by the needs of the national rail network, at least until Crossrail Two eventually allows Tramlink to take over the adjacent Platform 9. This will become possible when many suburban trains are diverted to new underground platforms, while immediately alongside the station stands the Centre Court shopping centre, preventing any further expansion to the side of the existing station.

Virtually the only paper ticket now issued for use on Tramlink is this one day bus & tram pass, issued by the ticket office at Wimbledon.

For many years, Wimbledon has been the biggest source of passenger disquiet on the Tramlink over the ticketing system, because tram ticketing is dealt with differently to every other stop on the system and every other service at Wimbledon. There are ticket gates at the entrance to the station itself, but there is also an Oyster/smartcard reader on Platform 10, and anyone using Tramlink with a smart card has to touch in both at the main entrance and on Platform 10.

Equally, if you got on a train at nearby Earlsfield station, for example, and have touched in there, when you get to Wimbledon you have to touch in again to get on the tram otherwise you are faced with a penalty fare. Elsewhere, Tramlink ticketing works like London buses, except that you touch in on the platform, not on the vehicle itself. But as if that was not confusing enough, passengers can also be caught out when they are thinking in 'train mode' and touch out with their smartcards on Platform 10, as they will then be charged twice for their journey!

Posters at nearby tram stops explain the complex situation, but many people still get caught that way and, according to an informed source, most of the time an inspector will simply allow the passenger to hop off at a tram stop and touch in again during their journey. Customer complaints about the ticketing situation at Wimbledon are said to outnumber all other complains to Tramlink put together, but where you have the tram and the train sharing a platform at a gated station there seems no easy solution.

Avoiding all the pitfalls of Tramlink ticketing at Wimbledon, and after the network went cashless on 16 July 2018, it is still possible to buy one paper ticket at the station for use on the system, a £5 London Bus & Tram Pass. This works out costing

London Bus & Tram Pass

Ticket type	Price
1DAY BUS&TRAM	£5·00M

Valid on

31·OCT·18   1089557834

Between		Number
WIMBLEDON *	& LONDON BUS&TRAM	85798

Route
BUS & TRAM ONLY

Printed 11:10 on 31·OCT·18

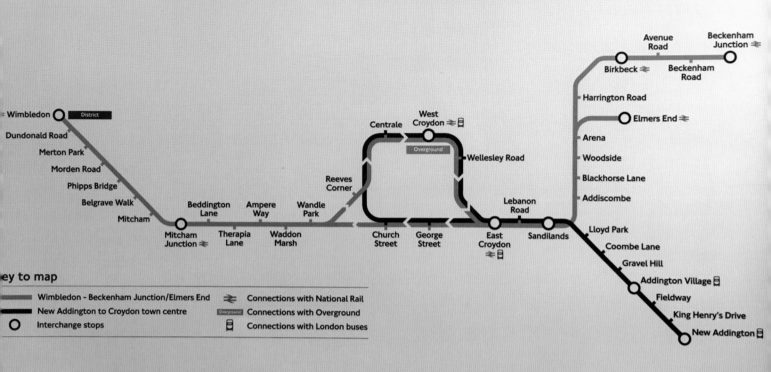

Key to map

▬▬▬	Wimbledon - Beckenham Junction/Elmers End	⇌	Connections with National Rail
▬▬▬	New Addington to Croydon town centre	Overground	Connections with Overground
○	Interchange stops	▤	Connections with London buses

A recent User Guide, featuring Stadler vehicle 2558 at Wimbledon station.

slightly more than the £4.50 daily cap on bus and tram fares using a smartcard, but for anyone taking a tour of the system, the 50p surcharge removes all the hassle of remembering to tap in at every stop before boarding a tram!

Setting out for Croydon, the single line of Tramlink passes under Wimbledon Bridge, carrying Wimbledon Hill Road before bearing round to the left where it immediately becomes double track and continues round to the first stop, *Dundonald Road*. One immediately noticeable feature on one of the two platforms here, as at every other stop, is the large bag shrouding the now disused ticket machine, following the abolition of cash fares on Tramlink in July 2018.

One unique feature of the system here is a sign on the northbound running line to the south of the stop, which orders a tram to halt if another tram is already in the stop, to avoid triggering the road crossing traffic lights. So if there is a tram in the stop heading for Wimbledon, a second tram would stop at this marker until the first one has cleared the stop. Without such an instruction, the second tram would activate the traffic lights and be blocking a busy road while waiting to get onto the stop.

A current map of the system, showing interchanges with bus and rail services. Photo courtesy of Transport for London.

2565 stands in platform 10a at Wimbledon on 31 October 2018 as 2557 departs platform 10b with a service to Beckenham Junction.

2548 at Dundonald Road on 31 October 2018 with a Beckenham Junction service.

Having crossed Dundonald Road, which is the first of many traffic light-controlled level crossings on the system, the route straightens out before another even busier road crossing where the line crosses the A238 Kingston Road at its junction with the B285 Hartfield Road, and is subject to three-way control by traffic lights. Standing at the Merton Park stop nearby and seeing a police van on an emergency call pull out immediately in front of an approaching tram was a reminder of just how open the system is, and the ease with which accidents can occur.

Merton Park was the first station on the former Wimbledon–West Croydon railway line and was also once a junction for a line to Merton Abbey and Tooting, which had closed to freight in 1972 but had lost its passenger services as long ago as 1929. No evidence remains apart from a footpath heading along the line of its former route. Continuing round a left-hand bend and then in a fairly straight south-easterly direction, the double track section comes to an end immediately south of the next stop, *Morden Road*. Here a bridge carrying the A24 Morden Road stands alongside what was a second station on the railway line, where there had been a single platform.

There now follows a pleasantly rural stretch of line as the single track passes over two bridges spanning the River Wandle, once famed for supplying water to the former Young's Brewery in Wandsworth, and alongside the large

2545 approaches Morden Road on 31 October 2018 with a service to Elmers End.

2545 heads onto the single track south of Morden Road on 31 October 2018.

Morden Hall Park. The 2008 *Horizon* study examined doubling this stretch of the line, but the problem is that it runs alongside protected wetlands at the back of the National Trust-owned Park, with the wetlands actually extending to within the tramway's boundary fence.

The line then becomes double track once again as it approaches its next stop, *Phipps Bridge*. Here there are the first of two successive island platforms, with the stop only being accessible by footpaths to a nearby housing estate north of the line and the park to the south.

From Phipps Bridge it is possible to see the next stop, *Belgrave Walk*, only a short distance further on. This second island platform also serves the residential area immediately to its north, with the remains of what was once an extensive industrial area just beyond the stop. The double track alignment continues from here almost as far as *Mitcham* where there is a short section of interlaced track as the line passes under a bridge carrying

the A217 London Road. Here the track width is limited by a series of concrete blocks, which date from the collapse of a retaining wall north of the line in the 1960s and would be no easy matter to remove.

Another feature of the 2015/6 enhancement works was a doubling of the section south from Mitcham station, almost as far as the next stop, *Mitcham Junction*, although fitting the tramway under a road bridge on the A237 Carshalton Road, spanning the Wimbledon route and the adjacent national railway double track route, means another section of single line at this point, before reaching the stop alongside the two platforms of Mitcham Junction station. One feature of the doubled section from Mitcham is that a speed restriction on it is more severe than in the days when it was a single line, reflecting the increasingly cautious approach of TfL that has also seen the system's maximum speed reduced from 80 to 70km/h.

Belgrave Walk on 31 October 2018, with 2537 bound for Wimbledon and 2556 for Beckenham Junction.

2560 heads onto the section of inter-laced track north of Mitcham on 31 October 2018 with a service for Wimbledon.

2546 approaches Mitcham on 31 October 2018 with a Wimbledon service.

2553 descends from the single track Mitcham flyover on 31 October 2018 with a Wimbledon service.

Continuing on in a south-easterly direction from Mitcham Junction, the route becomes single track once again as it climbs steeply to cross the railway lines on a single span steel girder bridge with concrete supports, before double track resumes and the route heads in a straight line, with Mitcham Golf Course on each side, as it approaches its next stop, *Beddington Lane*, and the edge of what was once the industrial heart of the Wandle Valley, but has now become an important out-of-town retail area. Like Morden Road, this was previously a single platform station on the former railway route.

From the platforms at Beddington Lane it is possible to look beyond a level crossing of the B272 Beddington Lane and down the line ahead to the western end of the Therapia Lane depot. As the site it occupies is relatively narrow (80 metres), the running lines curve round to the left to skirt the depot on its eastern side, with a crossover and single line access to the depot from the Beddington Lane direction to enable trams from the depot to head in the Wimbledon direction.

After passing short staff platforms on each side of the line (which have never been used), the route passes the main depot entrance, with a single access line and a crossover that allows tram services from Wimbledon to terminate at the *Therapia Lane* stop, as happens at the end of each day's service, and then reverse back into the depot. Another section of

2557 heads away from Beddington Lane for Wimbledon on 31 October 2018 and passes 2534 on an Elmers End service.

The last tram in the fleet (2565) arrives at Ampere Way on 31 October 2018 with an Elmers End service.

2557 approaches Waddon Marsh on 31 October 2018 with a service for Beckenham Junction.

straight line brings you to *Ampere Way*, a stop whose name reflects its industrial past and from where the dominant architectural features are two huge chimneys on the site of the former power station, now adorned with the livery of IKEA, whose store is on the site, along with a huge empty gas holder on the opposite side of the line, close to the next stop, *Waddon Marsh*.

This stop is some way to the south of the A23 Purley Way, which the line passes underneath, the former railway station having stood to the north side of the road bridge, closer to nearby housing. Like Ampere Way however, the main focus of the present day stop is the extensive retail area, with a large Decathlon sports store and an equally large Sainsbury's superstore located immediately to the south of the tram stop.

One final stop before the line enters central Croydon is at *Wandle Park*, to the south of the attractive looking park and in an area that has seen a significant level of new housing development in recent years. This is then followed by another section of single line as the route ascends onto its main architectural feature, the Wandle Park flyover, which carries it over the Sutton to West Croydon railway line before descending and running parallel with the railway for a short distance, then taking a sharp right hand turn to enter the stop at *Reeves Corner*.

Scott McIntosh recalls how controversial the planned flyover proved to be with local residents, particularly one proposal to shield it from nearby houses with a brick wall: 'This was a very run-down area

2534 rounds Reeves Corner on 31 October 2018 with a Wimbledon service.

when we were doing the development work and the houses were pre-gentrification and scruffy. But the problem was that a modern concrete viaduct is not the prettiest thing to look at and the people in these houses were complaining that the noise of the trams would make their houses unsaleable. The fact that at the time they looked out across the road onto an electrified railway with eight-car trains passing every ten minutes did not seem to have sunk in!

'What we proposed was that, as the tracks rose towards the flyover we would put a wall in – a stepped brick wall which would just come up to hand-rail height on the tram track and would be built in a wave form, so that it would be self-buttressing, and there would be planting

2538 has just left Church Street stop on 31 October 2018 and is about to turn right towards West Croydon with a New Addington service.

in it. The 'Great Berlin Wall of Croydon' they called this! No, not having that – our houses will be ruined and we will never be able to live here.

'We did point out that this wall would effectively baffle all the noise from the railway as well as the trams, so the place would actually be quieter than it was at the time, but they were not having it; so again, as part of the project's cost-cutting, this wall was deleted by the private sector contractor and we were left with this rather messy area, whereas it could have been quite an attractive piece of wall.'

Shortly before the turn to Reeves Corner, the line splits just before passing under the A236 Roman Way and a sharp right-hand bend that heralds the start of street running as it joins Cairo New Road. The

tram stop here is only served by eastbound trams, while those heading towards Wimbledon or round the central Croydon loop serve a nearby stop in *Church Street*. In the event of disruption to central Croydon however, it is now possible to reverse trams arriving from Wimbledon at Reeves Corner.

Bearing sharply round to the left, the street-running central section of the line takes trams up Tamworth Road to the newest stop on the system, *Centrale* [see Chapter 5]. This is unique on the system in being located between two lanes of traffic, with a platform only on the right-hand side and the tram lane not restricted solely for use by trams.

From Tamworth Road the tramway extends into Station Road to serve the important interchange stop at *West Croydon*. This stands on the left-hand side of the road, adjacent to the bus station and with a nearby entrance to the National Rail/London Overground station, which was once terminus of the rail service from Wimbledon.

What is the system's most complex section of line comes next, as trams take a sharp right turn that puts them in the centre of the extremely busy A212 Wellesley Road – the principal north-south thoroughfare through Croydon – travelling in a straight section at the centre of the road before crossing to the left under traffic light control at the approach to an underpass and serving the stop at *Wellesley Road*. As if the road crossings were not enough, a 'Ransom Strip' and barrier behind the stop

2564 pauses at Centrale on 31 October 2018 with an Elmers End service.

West Croydon on 31 October 2018 with 2563 bound for Beckenham Junction.

2535 in Wellesley Road on 31 October 2018 with an Elmers End service.

mean that there is very limited space – the pavement being only just over two metres wide, creating a nightmare for pedestrians when the stop is busy.

Central Croydon

Westbound trams arriving at East Croydon continue along George Street as it passes over the Wellesley Road underpass then enter a narrow section of the road to pause at the *George Street* stop, which stands on the north side of the pavement just west of The George pub in a narrow section of the road where other vehicles can only stop in marked laybys.

They then follow an S-shaped bend as they cross the High Street and descend Crown Hill before bearing round to the right and reaching the *Church Street* stop,

which is also on the north side of the road. This is just a few feet short of the points, where trams bound for West Croydon bear round to the right and into Tamworth Road, while those heading for Wimbledon continue straight ahead over the traffic light-controlled junction, then turn right to pass the Reeves Corner stop.

Croydon–Elmers End

Eastbound trams that have left the Wellesley Road stop continue up the slip road parallel to the underpass, where the tramway bears sharply left at a junction with George Street to re-join the westbound line that heads into central Croydon along George Street, and uphill to reach the system's most important stop and interchange at *East Croydon*.

2530 at East Croydon on 6 November 2018 with an Elmers End service.

Here there are three platform faces, with eastbound services using the one closest to the station entrance and westbound trams for Wimbledon and West Croydon using the furthest, while the central platform sees use as an emergency turn-back, with points at either end of the stop giving access to it from each running line.

Heading down onto Addiscombe Road from East Croydon on what is initially a tram-only reservation, the first road junction is one with Cherry Orchard Road. This is one of the longstanding headaches for Tramlink, as it is prone to flooding, which in turn leaves debris in the form of grit on the track, creating issues of slipping for the tram vehicles. The track here has been replaced on a couple of occasions, but it remains an unresolved issue.

The tramway then follows Addiscombe Road as it winds its way towards the *Lebanon Road* stop, with traffic on the narrow road restricted to buses and vehicles accessing the numerous sideroads, but not to any through traffic. Given the tight clearance, the stops here have been staggered, with the westbound stop passed first before an eastbound tram reaches its platform and bus laybys being located opposite each tram stop.

From Lebanon Road the route continues due east through what is now a quiet residential area, not a major thoroughfare, before crossing the busy Chepstow Road intersection and entering a section of gently rising reserved track that runs parallel to Addiscombe Road and leads to the *Sandilands* stop. There have been

2561 at Lebanon Road stop on 6 November with a service for Wimbledon.

constant problems at the Chepstow Road junction with cars trying to follow trams and there has been a dispute between Croydon Council and the Department for Transport over the appropriate signage, with motorists failing to understand the blue 'bus only' or 'tram only' signs but the DfT rejecting the use of 'No Entry' signs.

As the man who originally developed the Tramlink scheme while at London Transport, Scott McIntosh is proud on how the system has transformed the Addiscombe Road area:

'From Chepstow Road to Church Street on the other side of Central Croydon we have a tram and bus mall all the way. It is one of the biggest public-transport-only corridors in the country, apart from the side roads, of course, where you are allowed to come out of any of them and drive along the road, but you cannot exit at either end, so you can go down one, along, then up one of the others. This has made it an exceptionally pleasant environment.'

McIntosh recalls how creating space for the tramway at Sandilands threw up a number of challenges, not least the resident of one of the few houses which Tramlink needed to acquire to take over their back gardens for the tram alignment: 'There was a woman who lived in one semi-detached property who was slightly mad and operated an unofficial squirrel sanctuary in her garden – she fed them and gave them names and insisted on telling the Parliamentary Committee in the two and a half days she gave evidence that the squirrels would all be devastated.

'The other owners simply said, what do we get? We told them full market price plus 15% plus all their removal expenses, so they immediately signed up to sell. But this one drove us mad. In the end we bought the two houses, using one as a site office, and sold the other on to a developer who turned it into flats and sold each one for more than we paid for the whole house in the first place.'

2557 approaches Sandilands from the Chepstow Road crossing lights on 6 November 2018 with an Elmers End service.

It was the presence of housing at Sandilands which necessitated the route of Tramlink to then descend a short and steep gradient to a point where the New Addington route splits from the one heading north to Beckenham Junction and Elmers End. This required ninety degree radius curves in each direction, to bring the tramway onto the alignment of the former Elmers End–Selsdon railway, and it was at this point that the worst accident in Tramlink's history occurred on 9 November 2016 [see Chapter 9].

Having descended the gradient and turned left under a bridge carrying Addiscombe Road, the tramway follows the railway cutting before crossing Bingham Road and entering the *Addiscombe* stop. The railway had been on

an embankment at this point, but, after bridges taking it over Bingham Road and nearby Lower Addiscombe Road had been removed, it was decided to remove the former railway embankments and run Tramlink at street level for greater accessibility.

The Addiscombe stop is some half a mile east of the former Addiscombe station (closed in 1997) and is built on the site of what had been Bingham Road station. That station was being little used by local residents when it finally closed in 1983, but the present-day tram stop is very visible between the two road crossings and there is even a popular nearby coffee shop called 'The Tram Stop'.

Apart from removal of the former railway embankment here, another

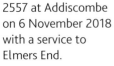

2557 at Addiscombe on 6 November 2018 with a service to Elmers End.

2562 departs
Blackhorse Lane on
6 November 2018
with a Wimbledon
service.

difficulty encountered by Tramlink was just north of this point at a place called Teevan Close. Here a developer had built flats on the former railway alignment, having only won consent on appeal, after opposition from both Croydon Council and LT. With the benefit of hindsight Minister Nicholas Ridley should never have permitted the development to go ahead, when he had been warned about its impact on Tramlink, and their purchase and subsequent demolition added an unnecessary £2-3m of costs to the project.

Regaining the original trackbed the route passes under *Blackhorse Lane* to serve a stop of the same name, bearing round to the right and passing the site of the former Addiscombe branch line junction, before reaching that line's only intermediate station, *Woodside.* Here the street-level station building survives, along with the original station steps down to the northbound side of the tram stop. This station building could find a new use if plans come to fruition for new depot

facilities, with a patch of land alongside the route being capable of holding around ten 30-metre trams, should the Tramlink fleet be further expanded, so giving the station buildings potential use for staff accommodation and a booking-on point.

Passing under the bridge carrying Spring Lane and the old station building, the tramway continues in a straight north-easterly direction until it reaches *Arena*, at the southern tip of South Norwood Country Park and named after the nearby Croydon Arena. This is home to a local football team, Croydon FC, who adopted 'The Trams' as their nickname when the system opened in 2000, where at one stage a hand bell-wielding supporter would ring it, and at the sound of the 'ding ding' the crowd would chant 'come on you Trams!'

Immediately north of Arena the Beckenham Junction line diverges to the left, while the double track alignment towards Elmers End continues for one tram length beyond the junction before becoming single line. At the time of recent

2538 is about to pass under the old station building at Woodside on 6 November 2018 with a service for Beckenham Junction.

2543 comes off the Beckenham Junction route at Arena on 6 November 2018 with a service for Wimbledon.

infrastructure upgrades there had been plans to extend the double track, as the route stands on what had previously been a double track railway, but instead a rather curious alternative was adopted in the form of a passing loop that has the effect of slowing trams down even when, as is usually the case, trams are not passing each other at this point.

Another change made on this section has been removal of a facility that allowed the double banking of trams in the single platform at *Elmers End*. In the past, if there were two trams running in quick succession, the first one arrived in Elmers End stop as the second one arrived in the double to single junction north of Arena. Then, instead of being forced to wait for the first tram to clear the station platform, the second tram could be signalled into the platform behind the first tram.

Elmers End station gives Tramlink passengers a cross-platform connection with South Eastern suburban services running from Hayes to London (Cannon Street or Charing Cross), with the Hayes line coming in from the right as the tramway serves the western platform (1), previously served by shuttle services to Addiscombe and Sanderstead, and where the track level has been raised to give level entry and exit from trams to the station platform.

Arena–Beckenham Junction

Diverging from the Elmers End route immediately north of the Arena stop, the double track route towards Beckenham Junction curves initially round to the left, passing the Arena itself, before a steady climb and series of further curves, where track stability has long been an issue, along the southern edge of South Norwood Country Park. It then crosses a private road giving access to Beckenham Crematorium as it enters the *Harrington Road* stop. A large warning sign for road users instructs them not to cross the tramway

Journey's end for 2536 on 6 November 2018 in platform 1 at Elmers End station.

2543 arrives at Harrington Road on 8 November 2018 as 2542 departs for Beckenham Junction.

when the crematorium gates (immediately beyond the southbound line) are closed.

Harrington Road marks the end of double track on the route towards Beckenham, with the line becoming single on the brow of a hill just one tram length north of the stop. From here the single line continues to ascend and bears sharply right to join the Crystal Palace to Beckenham Junction railway line. This had conveniently been reduced to single track in 1983, so Tramlink follows the former up (westbound) line for the rest of its route to Beckenham Junction.

Shortly after joining the railway alignment comes the stop at *Birkbeck*, where the extensive Beckenham Crematorium can be seen south of the stop and has another entrance nearby. Here the rather infrequent (and unreliable) train service now calls at the former down platform on the north side, while trams serve a much lower platform on the south side, with a chain link fence separating the two running lines and the only tram/

train interchange being via the Elmers End Road under-bridge to the eastern end of the station/tram stop.

The area of Victorian and Edwardian housing which Tramlink's original champion at LT, Scott McIntosh, had identified as being prime commuter territory is well served by Tramlink's next stop, *Avenue Road*. Here there was sufficient space in the railway alignment to fit in a passing loop with platforms on each side. Access to the stop is from Blandford Road, which runs parallel to the line all the way from Birkbeck, and, once again, there is a chain link fence extending well beyond each end of the stop to prevent tram users from straying onto the third-rail electrified railway line alongside.

The straight alignment, running in a north-easterly direction, continues as far as the next stop, *Beckenham Road*, where a single platform stop to the south of the line has been built on the railway embankment just east of a bridge carrying the lines over Beckenham Road. It stands close to Clock

2542 arrives
at Birkbeck on
8 November 2018
with a service for
Wimbledon.

2561 enters the
loop and stop at
Avenue Road on
8 November 2018
with a service for
Wimbledon.

2534 leaves Beckenham Road on 8 November 2018 and is about to pass 2545 which is entering the passing loop with a Wimbledon service.

The confined approach to Beckenham Junction terminus is evident here as 2531 departs on 8 November with a service to Wimbledon.

House station, the Hayes Line station immediately north of Elmers End, but like Beckenham Junction is not well situated for Beckenham town centre. At the time of Tramlink's original development Bromley Council would have nothing to do with an on-street tramway in Beckenham, a view that has almost certainly changed given Tramlink's successful growth over the past two decades.

Immediately beyond Beckenham Road stop comes one final passing loop, controlled by simple spring-loaded points, before the line bears gently round to the right as the main railway route from London Victoria comes in from the north. There is then a very tight access to the terminal platforms at *Beckenham Junction*, which involves a steep ascent and curve past an electricity sub-station to reach the stop on the south side of the small station car park. Here there is an island platform, allowing one tram to depart moments after another has arrived.

Sandilands-New Addington

What must be the most scenic section of Tramlink is the route heading south and then east from the busy Addiscombe Road at Sandilands towards Addington Village on the important New Addington route. This diverges from the Elmers End/Beckenham Junction routes by taking the south-facing right angle bend just east of the Sandilands stop that was the scene of the tragic November 2016 crash.

Lessons and legacies of that fatal accident are featured in chapter 9, but visible signs to the passenger today are the 20km/h speed restriction signs, large yellow and black chevrons to warn drivers of the junction, and in the East Croydon-bound direction the series of speed restrictions that take the maximum permitted speed down from 70km/h to 60km/h, then 40km/h and finally 20km/h as the bend approaches.

Coming off this sharp bend in the New Addington direction, the route immediately straightens as it joins the alignment of the former Elmers End–Sanderstead railway and enters the first of three tunnels that take the line beneath Radcliffe Road and Park Hill Rise. At the time of Tramlink's construction the tunnels were refurbished, with lighting installed, so that in the event of an emergency, passengers can be evacuated from a tram vehicle and walk out under the lighting.

Autumn colours in Lloyd Park on 8 November 2018, where 2548 departs for New Addington as 2535 approaches with a West Croydon service.

Emerging from the southern end of the three tunnels the route passes a new housing development built on the site of Coombe Road station, where one house had to be demolished during construction, before taking a sharp left-hand bend on the approach to the *Lloyd Park* stop. When they were first delivered, the newer Stadler Variobahn trams were unable to negotiate the combination of horizontal and vertical curves at this point, so it had to be lifted out and completely remodelled during a week's closure of the line. On visits in November 2018 and again in January 2019, it was noticeable that only Bombardier trams were being used on New Addington services.

From this stop onwards to Addington Village and New Addington, Tramlink is a classic continental line-side light railway,

initially ascending through attractive wooded countryside alongside the A212 Coombe Road, and later Coombe Lane. There is an access to the park adjacent to the Lloyd Park stop and, in keeping with its rural location, the original plan was for the track to have been grassed over along this stretch, but that proposal was disappointingly dropped when the line was built.

One attractive feature to have been adopted was the retention of a walking trail alongside the tramway, segregated from it only by a low wooden fence. 'It is a tramway and doesn't have to have two metre-high chain link fencing on both sides,' Scott McIntosh asserts. 'This was a horse riding trail, so we even have a pedestrian crossing over the tramway, which has a pelican crossing and an extra

2549 has completed the ascent from Lloyd Park and descends towards Coombe Lane stop on 8 November 2018 bound for New Addington.

button higher up, so you can stay on your horse and press it. We wanted to show that you can ride a horse next to a tramway, it's not frightening for a horse to encounter a tram!'

Beyond Lloyd Park the line climbs steadily and passes through the grounds of Geoffrey Harris House, which dates from 1761, that is now a care home for people with mental health and learning difficulties. After crossing Oaks Road the line then passes to the south side of the attractive Addington Hills. It is largely screened by trees from the parallel main road, before bearing left and reaching its next and remotest stop, *Coombe Lane*.

The line then continues its steep (8%) ascent before crossing the A212 at the top of Gravel Hill, a place where original plans were changed when the system was finally constructed. 'We had originally planned a very short underpass at that top roundabout, both for grade separation and to ease the gradient considerably,' explains Scott McIntosh. 'That was deleted by the private sector, so we had to incorporate a climb up to the road level and that does mean that in climbing up to this point the tram is at the theoretical limit of its adhesion capabilities.'

Having completed the steep ascent to Gravel Hill, the line then makes an equally steep descent as it runs in open country along the south side of Gravel Hill, passing through the grounds of Heathfield, an attractive 18-acre park which is open to the public and features ornamental gardens, ponds and woodland walks. At the bottom of the hill, and just before crossing the main road once again, the line reaches

2537 approaches Gravel Hill on 8 November 2018 with a New Addington service.

2552 approaches Addington Village on 8 November 2018.

the *Gravel Hill* stop, where there is a sign directing pedestrians to Ruskin College a quarter of a mile away.

Crossing Gravel Hill for a second time, the line enters Addington Park before a sharp left-hand turn takes it onto a busy dual carriageway called Kent Gate Way, where it initially crosses to a central reservation then crosses to the eastern side of this road over a second traffic light-signalled junction. The line then bears to the right and ascends once again to reach the stop at *Addington Village*, where an adjacent bus station was built to create an important interchange with Tramlink.

After leaving the interchange, the tramway bears right to run alongside the Addington Court Golf Course and parallel to Lodge Lane, running along the southern side of this busy thoroughfare for the rest of the way up to New Addington. Along this section are two final stops, at the first of which, *Fieldway*, there are more local bus connections. From here the route continues its south-easterly alignment, passing over

a large roundabout before reaching the penultimate stop, *King Henry's Drive*.

A final section of line then continues along the centre of a road called Parkway until it reaches a health centre, which forces the tramway to be squeezed into a single line to the south side of the building before passing over a road crossing and terminating at a stop with an island platform and two tracks, standing alongside Central Parade and with a number of local bus stops in the vicinity. In its original planning, Tramlink would have continued onwards for around 300 yards to a point closer to the main retail area of New Addington, but that was abandoned on grounds of cost.

The health centre's location, and the consequential need for a section of single line around it, represents a constraint on expanding service frequencies. Croydon Council gave the land for free so that the health centre could be built there, but the NHS has said that even if it moves the health centre, it will charge a significant

2539 nears Fieldway on 8 November 2018 with a New Addington service.

Decommissioned ticket machines shrouded in blue covers are evident in this view of King Henry's Drive on 8 November 2018.

This section of single track on the approach to New Addington, as the line passes a health centre, is a constraint on increasing frequencies along this busy route.

The end of the line at New Addington, seen here on 8 November 2018, where 2553 waits before returning to West Croydon.

price to hand back the site, because it is valuable real estate. As a result, one aspect of the 2008 *Horizon* study was to look at creating a reversing facility at Addington Village, so that any additional services on the route could terminate there.

CHAPTER 8

ACCIDENTS AND INCIDENTS

y far the most serious incident to have occurred on Tramlink during its first 20 years of operation was the fatal crash at Sandilands on 9 November 2016, when 7 people were killed and 62 people injured as tram 2551 came off the rails while travelling at excessive speed round the sharp left-hand bend that leads from the Sandilands tunnels to the tram stop. Before considering that tragic accident, and the lessons learned from it, in the following chapter, it is worth looking first at the range of less serious accidents and incidents that have occurred since services began in May 2000.

Studying details of incidents during the first few years of operation, as extensively documented on the excellent unofficial Tramlink website, it is clear that there are many recurring scenarios, which fall into a number of distinct categories. First there are road traffic accidents (RTAs), usually involving a car driver taking a wrong turn or jumping a traffic light, but surprisingly often featuring mistakes by bus drivers. Then there are incidents involving pedestrians accidentally being hit by trams, and occasional suicide attempts.

Finally come four further categories, namely infrastructure or equipment

Control Room at Therapia Lane on 16 January 2019.

2531 and 2548 await attention at Therapia Lane on 16 January 2019.

failures, such as track, points and tram vehicles; natural disasters, such as high winds and extreme temperatures; acts of vandalism and 'tram surfing', which were particularly serious issues in the early years of Tramlink; and lastly what I would call the downright bizarre – incidents ranging from police cars or delivery drivers blocking the line, a youth getting his skateboard stuck on the rails, and even one instance of services being halted by a family of ducks walking along the track!

Looking back to the year 2000, the first major incident occurred some three months before Tramlink services began when, on 3 February 2000, a serious RTA at Reeves Corner involving a van passing a red light put tram 2542, which at that time carried the colours of the system's builders, Amey, out of action for several weeks. Later that same month another RTA, this time at Lebanon Road, saw a

motorist remarkably manage to hit two trams (2535 and 2549) at the same time, while the first incident of a tram striking a pedestrian occurred on 11 February 2000, when a drunken man was staggering along the central reservation of Wellesley Road at 07.00, escaping with no serious injury.

In the month that the system finally opened, the first failure of a tram in service came just one week after services to New Addington were launched on 10 May, when 2550, which had the honour of operating the first service from East Croydon, failed at Larcombe Close, just south of the Sandilands tunnels. Despite the renowned reliability of the Bombardier vehicles, the same tram then failed at Gravel Hill later in the opening month while working a late night New Addington service.

Vandalism had emerged as an issue for Tramlink in the months before opening, with a number of air gun attacks on trams, while shortly after the system opened local youths took to removing tramstop lettering to create new names for the stops.

A first fatality

It took only one month from opening of Tramlink for the system to record its first fatality. This occurred on Sunday, 18 June 2000, when tram 2539 struck a person who had jumped in front of it as it approached Fieldway stop. Evidence pointed to a suicide, but it was not conclusive enough, leaving a subsequent inquest jury to record an open verdict.

The first serious disruption to services came on Tuesday, 29 August 2000, when damage to the overhead power line brought tram 2548 to a halt near the Birkbeck stop, closing the Beckenham Junction line for several hours. Two days later (31 August) there was a repeat incident at the same location, this time requiring repair to the overhead line

and closure until the following day, with the cause eventually being identified as a design error in the overhead line equipment, together with track quality and the heat.

From troubles caused by summer heat, it was only another two months until the system was hit by more severe weather, when a storm in the early hours of Monday, 30 October 2000, led to trees falling onto the tracks. The route to Beckenham was blocked at Addiscombe, Wimbledon line services were disrupted at Merton Park, and the New Addington route was affected in the Sandilands tunnels, where one tree struck tram 2549 inside the tunnels. While other routes were able to restore services during the day, the New Addington route remained blocked until midnight, when 2549 was removed to the depot.

Rounding off an eventful first year's operations, a snow fall early on 28 December 2000 caused a 198 bus to slide into the back of tram 2542 in Addiscombe Road, while two days later

A plethora of warning signs for motorists and pedestrians at the Harrington Road entrance to Beckenham Crematorium.

(30 December) there was another and more severe tram/bus incident when 2530 scraped past a bus in Station Road, West Croydon, sustaining serious body damage and many broken windows, that would mean the tram being out of service for several months.

A fall in incidents

Once familiarity with the workings of a tram system started to grow among Croydon's car drivers and pedestrians, the number of incidents began to fall. In its 2002/3 Railways Annual Report, the Health & Safety Executive (HSE) noted that these had fallen in each year since operations began. For Tramlink the figures for 2000/1 were 44 incidents (38 being collisions with road vehicles) falling in 2001/02 to 36 (22), 2002/3 to 29 (19). These figures compared favourably to other UK light rail systems and showed a correlation between the amount of on-street mileage and the level of incidents.

A decade later, that correlation identified by the HSE was noted by one of those people brought in to manage the system's transition to TfL ownership. Analysing every incident that had taken place in 2013, he plotted where they all were: which were on shared running, which were on non-shared streets, and which ones were off-street. What was clear, he told me, was an inverse correlation – if 15% of the track is on-street and 85% is off-street, then 85% of accidents were on-street and 15% were off-street.

Although the total number of accidents on Tramlink dropped in the first three years of its operation, there was then something of a reverse, with the number of major accidents rising from just seven in 2000/2001 to eighteen between January 2003 and January 2004. By that date – and after almost four years' service – there had been a total of 111 'minor vehicular accidents' involving trams since 2000, 53 involving pedestrians and 18 'major vehicular accidents'.

Responding to these figures, Roger Harding, General Manager of TCL, told the *Croydon Advertiser*: 'We were conscious this time last year that we were getting more pedestrian accidents and, as a consequence, we started a safety campaign. Now we are planning to do the same again in the next few weeks, aimed at car drivers. To put things in context, we are looking at 186 accidents over four years. In those four years we have actually run 10 million kilometres, so that works out at about one accident every 54,000km.'

Vandalism and careless car drivers

Tramlink's first full year of operation (2001) got off to an eventful start when tram 2549 was attacked by vandals throwing rocks from Jubilee Bridge, near Reeves Corner, breaking several windows and injuring a young girl, before its replacement (2548) was itself smashed by bricks at the Purley Way bridge and also had to be taken out of service. The following month (February 2001) saw further incidents of vandalism, with tram windows smashed by a gang at Arena, another in the town centre, and on 3 March the trouble had spread to Addington, with windows smashed on two trams at King Henry's Drive on 3 March.

Incidents of cars dropping onto the ballasted track near the Sandilands stop had already become a regular problem, but the year 2001 also witnessed not one, but two occasions when car drivers brought the system to a halt by apparently trying to drive onto the Wandle flyover, the single track line taking trams over the railway line south of West Croydon station. The first of these was on 11 February 2001, when a Ford Mondeo belonging to a local minicab firm managed to reach the bottom of the flyover, some 20 metres beyond the end of the paving and the 'cattle grid' preventing access by pedestrians.

One eastbound tram was descending the flyover when it was forced to stop by the obstruction and another had left Church

2547 stands at Bingham Road level crossing on 27 September 2001 after an encounter with a Jeep. (Photo: Graham Cluer)

St and was stopped under Jubilee Bridge at the signal. Passengers left each of these vehicles and swopped to the other, which then returned to where it had come from, while police officers managed a process of retrieving the offending vehicle by using a tram to tow it clear, using slats lifted from the 'cattle grid', and then planks of wood borrowed from nearby scaffolding to get it back onto the paved track.

While that first incident had been caused when the minicab driver had blacked out, the second incident, on 15 September 2001 was alcohol-related. On this occasion the driver not only dropped onto the ballasted track, having wrongly followed the tramline under Jubilee Bridge rather than turning left, but then managed to continue for more than 150m up the ballasted track to stop well up the incline of the flyover!

A tram surfing fatality

Besides throwing ballast and bricks at passing trams, another cause of needless problems for Tramlink was the highly dangerous practice of 'tram surfing', where youths would jump onto the rear of a tram, standing on the tow-bar cover and holding onto the windscreen wiper blades, where they were almost impossible to detect by a tram driver, especially when it was busy.

The first recorded incident and injury was at Waddon March on 29 December 2000, where a 19-year-old man fell from the back of a tram before being treated at the scene for his injuries then arrested by British Transport Police.

The first fatality from surfing occurred in the early hours of Sunday, 20 May 2001, when a 16-year-old youth from Beckenham fell from the back of a tram near Beckenham Road and struck his head. His body, which was subsequently run over by another tram whose driver didn't notice it, was discovered at 03.15 by a trespasser taking a short cut along the line, who alerted the authorities.

In an attempt to discourage tram surfing, the bottom of trams' windscreen wipers were coated in anti-vandal paint, with trams 2544, 2546 and 2551 being the first to be treated and have 'Warning - Anti-Vandal Paint' stickers next to the wiper. Despite the application of this semi-permanent and staining paint, the problem continued, with some surfers wrapping newspaper around the wiper blades to avoid contact with the paint.

At a subsequent inquest in December 2001, the coroner recommended fitting cameras so that tram drivers could see people surfing. Following this recommendation, TfL and TCL agreed to have two trams experimentally fitted with six cameras, one at each end to monitor the rear of the trams, as well as four in the saloon to monitor the passengers. These cameras would be linked to a monitor in each cab, with a recorder able to record for 33 hours at four frames per second normally, and in real time if the driver pressed a button to record an incident on disc, or sent images direct to the control room.

Two of the system's more bizarre incidents during its first full year involved ducks and a skateboard. On Monday, 16 July 2001, a mother duck took her ducklings for a walk up and down the single line between Beddington Lane and the Mitcham flyover between around 08.30 and 09.30, disrupting services until a wildfowl expert was called in to persuade

Engineers check damage to Nescafé-liveried 2533 after it had been hit by a car at Wellesley Road/ Poplar Walk junction on 10 March 2001. (Photo: Stephen Parascandalo)

mother duck it was not a good idea to take the family for a walk along the line.

Then on Sunday, 23 September 2001, a young boy aged around 8 attempted to skateboard across the tramline in Church Street in front of a tram. His stunt did not quite work however, with his skateboard hitting the kerb and throwing him into the doorway of the McDonalds restaurant, while the skateboard rolled back into the tram's path, jamming underneath it! After some delay, British Transport Police arrived, allowing the tram to reverse and the skateboard to be retrieved.

Tramlink's third fatality occurred at the same site as its first, Fieldway, when on Saturday, 7 September 2002, a 78-year-old great-grandmother from New Addington was struck by tram 2551 travelling towards New Addington as she crossed the foot crossing at the Croydon end of the stop. It is thought she was crossing to catch a Croydon-bound tram when she stepped out in front of the New Addington-bound tram. Fire and Ambulance crews were on the scene very quickly and the lady was taken to Mayday Hospital with serious head injuries, but was dead on arrival. The 30-year-old female tram driver was taken to Bromley Hospital suffering from shock

and TCL General Manager Roger Harding told the local press of his shock and sadness at the incident, with police treating it as a non-suspicious road traffic accident.

A fatality at Lloyd Park

The year 2002 saw another fatality on Tramlink when at 13.40 on 12 December 2002 tram 2534 heading towards Croydon from New Addington struck a person near the Lloyd Park Emergency Access crossing, just before the tram-stop. The tram windscreen was broken and it came to a stand about two tram lengths beyond the body. This was in an area with excellent visibility, with no bushes or large trees close to the tram, just open grass and a small, low wooden fence.

A delayed inquest into the fatality took place in November 2003. It heard how the victim, 34-year-old Frances Williams, had been involved in a serious car accident only a few weeks earlier. This had left her with serious head and neurological injuries, affecting her personality, and on the day of the accident she had insisted on leaving her parents' house, where she was recuperating, to go for a walk.

Tram driver Terence Hulme saw her walking towards the track but believed her not to be a threat. When he realised she was not going to stop, he applied the hazard brakes 28 metres before the impact – he was travelling at 40mph, slower than the 80km/h (50mph) line speed. In a statement after the accident, the driver said that the lady turned to look at the tram but showed no reaction on her face as she continued to walk into its path.

Sadly, the highly experienced tram driver, who had been praised for his actions in an earlier incident involving a bike being thrown in front of his tram, died suddenly in February 2003, shortly after he had been passed to return to driving duties following the accident. In his summing up, the Coroner said: 'But for the road accident previously, she wouldn't have come to this unhappy end. I'm sure if the driver could

A Ford Fiesta has taken a wrong turn at Sandilands on 24 September 2002. (Photo: Stephen Parascandalo)

be here today to tell his story he would say that he had no idea something terrible was going to happen until the very last minute.' The jury recorded a verdict of Accidental Death.

In an attempt to make Tramlink safer, Transport for London launched a Safety Campaign on 22 June 2003, urging people to Mind their Step when around the system. Posters appeared on trams and tram stops and advertisements were published in local newspapers. London Mayor Ken Livingstone said, 'Croydon Tramlink has an extremely low accident rate, which is quite an achievement considering trams have only been reintroduced to London's streets relatively recently. But we can't afford to be complacent and this campaign will remind people in Croydon to take that extra bit of care when crossing the tracks.'

But tragedy struck once again, on the same day that the campaign was launched, when tram 2531 travelling from Beckenham Junction fatally struck 57-year-old Rex Nicholson of Croydon on the pedestrian crossing of Addiscombe Road at the Chepstow Road junction. It was thought that he ignored the Red Man and crossed behind an eastbound tram, walking into the path of 2531 going westbound. Tram drivers are trained to sound the bell as they pass other trams on street-running sections – on this occasion the warning was not effective.

Incidents at Phipps Bridge

One Tramlink location to have featured in two Rail Accident Investigation Branch (RAIB) enquiries is the Phipps Bridge tram stop, where derailments occurred on Friday, 21 October 2005, and then again on Thursday, 26 May 2006. What appears slightly worrying is that in both cases the RAIB said that the immediate cause was the tram driver not reacting to a track-side warning that the points were incorrectly set and failing to stop the tram before reaching the points.

On the first occasion (10.38 on 21 October 2005), tram 2530 was travelling eastbound on the single line between Wimbledon and Croydon with approximately 45 passengers on board. It derailed as it passed over points at the single to double line junction and came to rest 37 metres beyond the points, with no injuries sustained, and the passengers were evacuated to the adjacent tram stop by the driver and other staff. Following repairs to minor track damage, normal services were reinstated at 21.10 hrs on the same day.

Contributing factors to the accident were identified by RAIB as being failure of the points to return to normal after the passage of the previous tram; failure of the control room staff to alert drivers to the malfunction of the points; and the poor clarity of the points position indicator display when the points were not set correctly. Recommendations made to reduce the likelihood of a recurrence covered assessing and improving the clarity of the points indicator when points were not correctly set; a review of the inspection and maintenance regime for the points; a joint review of the system for dealing with alarms in the control room; and a review of control room procedures as soon as was practicable to ensure that controllers responded promptly and appropriately to each incident.

Seven months later, at 15.57 on Thursday, 25 May 2006, tram 2532, travelling eastbound between Wimbledon and Croydon with around 180 passengers on board derailed on the approach to Phipps Bridge tram stop. As the tram approached the points, they had remained, incorrectly, in the reverse position after the last tram had passed in the opposite direction. After the leading bogie of the tram had passed over them the points sprang back into the normal position. With the front and rear of the tram diverging, the centre bogie derailed. There were no injuries caused by the derailment.

In the case of the May 2006 accident, RAIB determined that causal factors were the points not returning to their normal position following the passage of the previous tram; the points then changing position as the tram passed over them; and the poor visibility of the indicator display when the points were not set correctly. RAIB made two recommendations as a result of the report, aimed at ensuring the competence of staff working on points mechanisms and instructing Tramlink's operators to ensure that the training given to new drivers was keeping risks as low as was reasonably practicable.

A bad week for TfL

Shortly after the takeover of Tramlink by TfL in 2008, a period of several years which had seen relatively few serious incidents on the system came to an abrupt end when there were two fatal accidents within the space of a week in September 2008. This put what boss at the time Phil Hewitt describes as 'a huge strain on the new team'. The first of these occurred on 7 September 2008 when a route 468 bus passed a red traffic light and collided with tram 2534 in George Street, causing one fatality. The driver of the bus was later convicted of causing death by dangerous driving and sentenced to four years in prison.

The second incident took place on Saturday, 13 September 2008, when tram 2530, travelling at 62km/h, collided with a 21-year-old cyclist at Morden Hall Park footpath crossing between the Morden Road and Phipps Bridge tram stops. The cyclist sustained injuries and later died, with the incident leading to another RAIB investigation and the issue of an Improvement Notice.

'This led to some changes in how the network was managed, because we found that changes had been made to the network that no-one was aware of and footways had been modified,' recalls Hewitt. 'It was quite sobering to get to that position and led to improvements which were cascaded upwards, and nationally as well as a result, so although they were terrible things to happen you can learn from them and do things better.'

In its investigation, RAIB identified that the immediate cause of the accident was that the cyclist rode onto the crossing without looking at the approaching tram. Causal factors were that the cyclist may

The driver of this van has had a lucky escape after being hit by 2554 at Bingham Road level crossing on 29 March 2003.
(Photo: Graham Cluer)

2540 has been derailed at King Henry's Drive on 28 May 2003 after colliding with a bus while on its line 3 journey to West Croydon.

have been wearing headphones, which prevented him hearing the audible warnings sounded by the tram driver, and that the layout of the approach to the crossing did not encourage cyclists to look towards eastbound trams. Crucially, the investigation found that a possible contributory factor was that the risks created by the way Morden Hall Park and other foot crossings on Tramlink were being used had not been assessed by the infrastructure manager since opening.

As a consequence of this accident, RAIB has made one recommendation targeted at Tramtrack Croydon Ltd (trading as London Tramlink), the owner and infrastructure manager, to modify footpath crossings on their system where appropriate. Following the accident, the Office of Rail Regulation (ORR) issued an Improvement Notice requiring Tramtrack Croydon Ltd to assess the risks to users at footpath crossings on its system, and identify any further actions required to reduce risk.

This assessment was duly carried out by the required date, 14 January 2009, and Tramtrack Croydon Ltd drew up a programme of works for improvements at a number of pedestrian crossings. This work involved the modification of crossings, 'so that users are influenced to look both ways before crossing, and cyclists are encouraged to slow down sufficiently (by means such as the provision of barriers, signs and/or markings), to give them time to become aware of approaching trams.'

A derailment at East Croydon

After the lessons learned at Morden Hall, it would be three and a half years until Tramlink once again came under the RAIB spotlight, this time for very different reasons and thankfully not leading to any casualties. This was an incident early on the morning of 17 February 2012, when a westbound tram derailed after passing over facing

A safety booklet aimed at children and featuring a character called Tramlink Tom, who teaches them how to use the system safely.

points as it approached the platform at East Croydon. The tram was running one minute behind the tram ahead, and was routed left to follow it towards Platform 3. As the tram travelled forwards at low speed, the points moved under its leading bogie, forcing its centre and rear bogies right towards Platform 2. The centre bogie derailed as the routes diverged. Approximately 100 passengers were detrained close to the platform, with no reported injuries.

The main cause of this accident was that a track circuit failed to respond to an approaching tram and lock the points to prevent movement. The track circuit was not correctly adjusted and the rail head may have been contaminated with silt. In its report, the RAIB made three recommendations to London Tramlink that focussed on operational and signalling arrangements, the control of silt and rail head contamination, and

track circuit settings. Firstly, Tramlink was to review the operational and signalling arrangements at East Croydon to consider whether undue reliance was being placed on the correct operation of track circuits.

Secondly, to reduce the risk of rail head contamination affecting the correct operation of track circuits, Tramlink was told that track inspections should be carried out immediately after events (such as heavy rain) which could lead to accumulation of silt. It was told it should identify areas of paved track where silt collected and instigate an improved inspection and cleaning regime where such silt might affect the safe operation of the tramway system. Thirdly, Tramlink was to, 'conduct a fundamental review of track circuit settings and wheel tyre to wheel tyre resistances and then put in place a system of maintenance that ensures the signalling equipment and trams are maintained to mutually compatible standards, which include due allowance for reasonably foreseeable levels of contamination at the wheel/rail interface.'

A pedestrian is hit at Sandilands

Three months after the East Croydon derailment, Tramlink again came under RAIB scrutiny following an incident on 16 May 2012 when a pedestrian was struck by a tram as she crossed the tramway on a foot crossing at the approach to the Sandilands stop. The impact resulted in the pedestrian falling into the space between the platform and the tram where she remained trapped as the tram continued into the platform, and suffered serious injuries. In its investigation, RAIB found that the pedestrian had not looked for an approaching tram before she crossed. However, it noted that there was a possible obstruction to the pedestrian's view of approaching trams as she walked towards the entrance to the tram stop and the configuration of the crossing meant that she approached it with her back to trams running on the nearest track.

RAIB noted that risk assessments had been undertaken in relation to safety at Sandilands foot crossing (and other foot crossings on the Croydon tram network) in 2008/9 and 2011. But its investigation found that the methodology employed in the 2008/9 assessment was not a suitable basis for prioritising the foot crossings for safety improvements, noting that with agreement of the Office of Rail Regulation, Tramlink mainly prioritised crossings remote from tram stops for safety improvements from 2009 onwards (following the Morden Hall accident mentioned above). The 2011 risk assessment also identified that the foot crossing at Sandilands represented the highest risk of the fifty-two crossings that were considered in the review.

The accident report said Tramlink did not make any safety improvements to reduce the probability of a pedestrian being struck on the foot crossing at Sandilands in response to the 2011 findings. While it had taken some action to understand the risk at foot crossings on its network, and had introduced a speed restriction of 25 km/h for trams passing over foot crossings on the approach to all tram stops, Tramlink's processes for managing the risk at individual crossings were not effective. Two factors noted by RAIB as affecting the consequences of the accident were that the tram driver did not apply the hazard brake (which achieves a higher rate of retardation than the brake normally employed for stopping trams) after the tram struck the pedestrian and, secondly, that there was enough vertical and horizontal clearance to create a survival space for the pedestrian in the position where she fell.

Foremost of five RAIB recommendations following this incident was for Tramlink to improve its approach to foot crossing risk assessment, to clearly identify those locations where risk was highest, and also identify the factors that needed to be considered to reduce risk. This revised approach should consider all of the factors identified in the 2011 risk assessment and be extended to all foot crossings on the system. The RAIB said Tramlink, in conjunction with its operator, Tram Operations Ltd, should continue to develop its process for periodically assessing risk at all foot crossings, and also identified a requirement for tram drivers to be instructed in use of the tram's hazard brake when a tram has struck a pedestrian.

Doors open on a moving tram

Almost a year after the Sandilands pedestrian accident a highly unusual incident took place in virtually the same location when, on 13 April 2013, a Beckenham Junction-bound tram departed from the Lebanon Road and Sandilands stops with all of its doors open on the left-hand side. Some of the doors closed automatically during the journey, but one set of doors remained open throughout the incident. The incident ended when a controller monitoring the tram on CCTV noticed that it had departed from Sandilands with its doors open, and arranged for the tram to be stopped. Although there were no casualties, there was potential for serious injury.

In its report, the RAIB noted that the tram was able to move with its doors open because a fault override switch, which disables safety systems such as the door-traction interlock, had been inadvertently operated by the driver while trying to resolve a fault with the tram. The driver did not close and check the doors before departing from Lebanon Road and Sandilands, partly because he was distracted from dealing with the fault, and partly because he did not believe that the tram could be moved with any of its doors open. The design of controls and displays in the driving cab contributed to the driver's inadvertent operation of the fault override switch, while a breakdown in communication between driver and passengers, and between the driver and the controller, meant that neither was aware of the problem until after the tram left Sandilands.

Eight recommendations were made by the RAIB following this incident, of which four were directed at the First Group subsidiary, Tram Operations Ltd, which operates Tramlink, and were aimed at improving the design of tram controls and displays, as well as training of staff on, and processes for, fault handling and communications. Two recommendations were made to Tramlink, one (in consultation with Tram Operations Ltd) related to improving cab displays and labelling, and one on enhancing the quality of the radio system on the network. One recommendation was made to all UK tram operators concerning the accidental operation of safety override switches, while the final recommendation was to the Office of Rail Regulation regarding the provision of guidance on ergonomics principles for cab interface design.

Stadler vehicle 2555 had failed at Beckenham Junction on 8 November 2018, while 2531 is about to depart for Wimbledon.

CHAPTER 9

THE 2016 SANDILANDS DISASTER

A defining moment in the history of Tramlink was at 06.07 hrs on Wednesday, 9 November 2016, when tram 2551 approached the Sandilands junction with a New Addington–Wimbledon service. Having passed through the three Sandilands tunnels at the maximum permitted line-speed of 80km/h, the driver should have significantly reduced speed to just 20km/h to safely pass round the sharp left-hand curve, but instead tram 2551 was travelling at 73km/h as it passed the 20km/h speed limit sign.

The tram, with seventy people on board, overturned and slid 27 metres before coming to rest. Passengers were thrown around inside the tram, and some were thrown out of the vehicle and crushed by it. Seven people were killed and sixty-two were injured, many of them seriously, in Britain's worst tram disaster for almost a century. It was also the first accident involving fatalities among passengers on any of the country's new generation of tram and light rail systems.

Driver Alfred Dorris was arrested by British Transport Police on suspicion of manslaughter, but never charged. A subsequent RAIB investigation concluded that driver error was the cause of the accident, with Dorris probably

This view of Sandilands Junction on 8 November 2018 shows the large chevrons warning drivers of the sharp bend ahead. 2560 rounds the curve towards Sandilands as 2548 waits with a service from New Addington to West Croydon.

losing concentration during a 'microsleep'. There was no evidence that his health or fitness contributed to the crash, but he may have been 'fatigued' due to insufficient sleep – he had woken at 03.30 hrs that morning and had not had breakfast.

Eye-witnesses who spoke to *The Times* described the full horror of the accident, seeing bodies with severe head injuries, and wounded passengers covered in blood and screaming in pain. Rhys McCausland, 19, a chef, recalled being thrown across the carriage before his head was trapped against the track bed: 'I rolled on my back; the glass had smashed behind me and my face rolled over the gravel,' he said. 'There were people flying towards us and bags flying everywhere. It was quite dark at the time and it was still raining. I saw some horrific scenes – it was like something out of a nightmare.'

Another passenger on the ill-fated journey was Martin Bamford, who suffered broken ribs, whiplash and concussion, and who described the moment the tram flipped onto its side as 'carnage'. 'We hit the bend way too fast,' Mr Bamford, 30, from south London, said. 'The tram was full, mainly of people going to work. There was a girl who was on top of me and she did not look very much alive at all. She was bleeding all over the place. People had broken legs and head injuries.'

Speculation that driver fatigue and excessive speed were to blame for the crash arose immediately, and the sense of public concern at tram safety was exacerbated when reports emerged later that day that British Transport Police had received reports that another tram had nearly derailed at the same place only days before.

Earlier incidents at Sandilands

James Tofield, a bus driver, released a text message he sent to his fiancée on the morning of 31 October, saying his journey had been like 'a ride from Alton Towers'.

He said that the tram driver 'went round the bend so fast…smacked on the brakes and somehow managed to stay on the track'. Another passenger on that journey, Andy Nias, had posted an account on Facebook shortly after it happened. He wrote: 'Tram driver took the hard corner to Sandilands at 40mph!! I swear the tram lifted onto one side.'

Further adding to the unease was a report in *The Sunday Times* on 13 November 2016, 'Tram drivers feared "nasty bend"', which reported that police were investigating a third complaint of a tram being driven too fast. Cliff Gadd, 56, said it felt as if a 'racing driver' was in control of the tram he caught with his 9-year-old grand-daughter on 22 October, claiming it made a 'screaming' noise as it sped through a tunnel just before the sharp bend where Wednesday's derailment took place. 'I used to work on the railways and I know what too fast is and this was much too fast,' said Gadd, a delivery driver. He later remonstrated with the driver, accusing him of driving the tram recklessly, but claims the man laughed.

British Transport Police confirmed to *The Sunday Times* that officers were investigating Gadd's account, along with the two separate allegations that a tram almost came off the tracks on the same bend on 31 October. Meantime, a former tram driver with six years' experience criticised what he described as 'crazy' shift rotas that meant drivers were unable to get into regular sleep patterns. He claimed drivers had fallen asleep at the controls in the past and that the left-hand turn where the accident happened was known as a nasty bend. 'Nobody is ever fully awake,' he said. 'I was always feeling in a bit of a daze and that is because the way the shifts work doesn't allow the drivers to get a regular sleep pattern.'

Days later, Tim O'Toole, Chief Executive of FirstGroup, the parent company of Tramlink operator Tram Operations Ltd, dismissed suggestions that drivers' erratic shift patterns may have been a

contributory factor in the crash: 'The shifts and the timetables are set in co-operation with the employees and the trade unions, and the employees can put in bids for the shifts they prefer. This has just not been a subject that's been an active topic at Tramlink.' Speaking to *The Times* on the announcement of its interim results on 15 November 2015, the FirstGroup boss indicated his belief that investigators into the crash would recommend that light rail vehicles be fitted with automatic vehicle cut-out or braking systems.

A first report on the accident

An interim report from RAIB, published a week after the disaster, said that the tram had been travelling at 43.5mph as it entered the bend with its 20km/h (12mph) speed limit, and had found no evidence of brake problems or track defects. RAIB said that 'some braking' was applied on the long stretch of track leading up to the

corner when the tram was travelling at a maximum of 80km/h, but this was 'only sufficient' to reduce the tram's speed slightly by the time it entered the bend. Urgent safety advice was issued by RAIB to FirstGroup and TfL, with both urged to take measures to reduce the risk for trams approaching the location when the line reopened. This could include a further speed restriction before the start of the 20km/h limit and more warning signs.

Immediately following the disaster, tram services were suspended between East Croydon and Harrington Road, Addington Village and Elmers End to enable the British Transport Police and RAIB to thoroughly investigate the site and to allow TfL engineers to carry out repair work. As a precautionary measure, and in keeping with the RAIB's advice, TfL imposed a further speed restriction before the existing 20km/h section near Sandilands.

A 60km/h limit was introduced between the 80km/h limit on the straight stretch

Warning chevrons are clearly visible at the far end of Sandilands tunnels as 2563 emerges on 5 April 2019 with a New Addington service. Drivers heading towards Croydon are instructed to reduce speed from 70 to 60km/h at the tunnel entrance, then 40km/h mid-way through the tunnels and finally just 20km/h as they approach the sharp left-hand bend at Sandilands.

Ill-fated 2551 pauses at Beddington Lane on 13 March 2007 with a Line 3 service to New Addington. (Photo: Gareth Prior)

of line approaching Sandilands tunnels and the 20km/h limit. The 20km/h limit was also brought closer to the exit from the tunnels. Similar restrictions were implemented at three further locations on the tram network: in the opposite direction between Sandilands and Lloyd Park; on the approach to Sandilands from the Beckenham Junction/Elmers End branch; and on the bend between Birkbeck and Harrington Road.

A week after the tragedy, tram services resumed across the whole tram network on 18 November 2016. Before resumption and in accordance with advice in the RAIB's interim report into the derailment, additional speed restrictions and associated signage were introduced near Sandilands. These precautionary measures were also implemented at the three other locations on the tram network mentioned above. All tram drivers had been fully briefed before resumption and additional staffs from both TfL and FirstGroup were made available across the network

to provide support and information for customers and employees. FirstGroup also began carrying out enhanced speed monitoring across the tram network.

RAIB publishes its investigation report

When its full report was finally published in December 2017, key findings of the RAIB investigation were that there was no mechanism to monitor driver alertness or to automatically apply the brakes when the tram was travelling too fast; there was inadequate signage to remind drivers when to start braking or to warn that they were approaching the sharp curve; and that the windows broke when people fell against them, so many passengers were thrown from the tram causing fatal or serious injuries.

The RAIB's investigation concluded that it is probable that the driver temporarily lost awareness on a section of route on which his workload was low. It suggested

that as he regained awareness, the driver may have become confused about his location and direction of travel through the tunnels, while the infrastructure did not contain sufficiently distinctive features to alert tram drivers that they were approaching the tight curve.

To carry out its investigation, RAIB had employed a range of methods that included: obtaining data from the tram's on-board recorder and the tramway's signalling system; conducting tests on the tram's safety systems; using computer modelling to understand the minimum speed that would overturn a tram on the curve at Sandilands; reviewing the design of the infrastructure; reviewing the tramway's safety and risk management systems; interviews with people and organisations involved; and surveying tram drivers to understand how trams were being driven on the New Addington route.

Analysis by RAIB indicated that a tram approaching Sandilands junction on the long straight stretch of line from Lloyd Park and through the three tunnels at the (then) maximum speed of 80km/h (since reduced to 70km/h) would need to apply its full brakes 180 metres before the curve's speed restriction sign to bring its speed down to 20km/h by the time it reached the sign itself. In clear conditions during darkness RAIB concluded that drivers could see the curve and read the speed restriction sign from around 90 metres away with headlights on full beam and 60 metres with a dipped beam.

This is about 90-120 metres beyond the point at which a full-service brake application must start, in order for the tram to slow down sufficiently to safely negotiate the curve. But RAIB noted that there was no sign alongside the track to alert drivers that they needed to apply the brake, this being something that they were expected to know from their route knowledge. In the case of 2551, its on-tram data recorder shows that its service brake was not applied until 2.5 seconds before it reached the 20km/h restriction sign, and that its speed was only reduced from 79 to 73km/h by the time it passed the sign.

An aerial view of the crash scene and 2551 on its side.

A close-up view of 2551 and its smashed windscreen. (Photo: RAIB)

Commenting on the outcome of its investigation, Simon French, Chief Inspector of Rail Accidents at RAIB, said: 'We are recommending action in five main areas. The first is the use of modern technology to intervene when trams approach hazardous features too fast, or when drivers lose awareness of the driving task. Tramways need to promote better awareness and management of the risk associated with tramway operations.

'Work needs to be done to reduce the extent of injuries caused to passengers in serious tram accidents, and to make it easier for them to escape. There needs to be improvements to safety management systems, particularly encouraging a culture in which everyone feels able to report their own mistakes. Finally, greater collaboration is needed across the tramway industry on matters relating to safety… It is vital that the right action is taken to stop such a tragic accident from ever happening again.'

In total the RAIB made fifteen recommendations intended to improve safety and covering a range of areas relating to Tramlink's operation. These encompassed technology, such as automatic braking, and systems to monitor driver alertness; better understanding

the risks associated with tramway operations, particularly when the tramway is not on a road, and the production of guidance on how these risks should be managed; improving the strength of doors and windows; improvements to safety management systems, particularly encouraging a culture in which everyone feels able to report their own mistakes; improvements to the tram operator's safety management arrangements so as to encourage staff to report their own mistakes and other safety issues; reviewing how tramways are regulated; and creation of a dedicated safety body for UK tramways.

Responding to both the RAIB December 2017 accident report, and an addendum published in October 2018, which included a description of a Transport for London (TfL) audit of the Tram Operations Limited's (TOL) fatigue risk management system, TfL commented: 'We welcome these reports and have continued to work alongside the RAIB, the Office of Rail and Road (ORR) and FirstGroup, who operate the tram network, to ensure all of the recommendations outlined are met. We have made significant progress on the recommendations set out by the RAIB and have completed some of the most vital. We have also published our own investigative report.

2551 approaches
Wandle Park on
13 September 2007
with a Line 3 service
to New Addington.
(Photo: Gareth Prior)

'Since the incident we have introduced a wide range of additional safety measures to make sure such a tragedy can never happen again. These include new signage and warning systems for drivers, additional speed restrictions, enhanced speed monitoring and an upgrade of the CCTV recording system. An in-cab driver protection device is now fitted to every tram, meaning that any sign of driver distraction or fatigue results in the driver being alerted immediately.

'This is the first time such a device has been used in the rail industry in the UK and has been commended by the ORR. This system has been shared and demonstrated to the UK Tram industry for possible implementation on other tram networks.'

Implementing the fifteen RAIB recommendations

Looking in detail at the RAIB recommendations, its first was for the Office of Rail and Road (ORR) to work with the UK tram industry to develop a new body to enable more effective UK-wide cooperation on matters related to safety, and the development of common standards and good practice guidance. In a detailed update on its progress in implementing the RAIB reforms, TfL noted that this recommendation was for the wider industry, and was being led by UK Trams (the umbrella body representing the UK light rail industry) and ORR. It added that a steering group had been established, of which TfL was a key member, with a Safety Standards Board proposed to provide regulation and consistency of safety standards across the industry.

RAIB Recommendation Two was an all-embracing one, proposing that UK tram operators, owners and infrastructure managers should jointly conduct a systematic review of operational risks and control measures associated with the design, maintenance and operation of tramways. This would be part of the programme of work for the new Safety Standards Board, mentioned in the first RAIB recommendation, and as a first step

TfL, in collaboration with operator TOL, reviewed its route risk assessments and network risk model and shared these with the wider UK tram industry to help inform the basis for an industry-wide risk model.

Measures to automatically reduce tram speeds if they approached higher risk locations at speeds which could result in derailment or overturning was RAIB Recommendation Three, something which TfL had begun working on shortly after the November 2016 disaster. A tender was issued for a system on the London Tram network that would automatically apply the brakes should the speed limit be exceeded at high risk locations, to bring a moving tram to a controlled stop if it were to exceed the speed limit at a designated location, and automatically alert the operations control centre.

The new safety system, which was due to be fully implemented by December 2019, would initially be configured to high priority locations as suggested by RAIB, but have the flexibility to be introduced elsewhere on the tram network. Preparatory feasibility and scoping work for this system was shared by TfL with other tram owners and operators to assist in the development of a programme for installing similar suitable systems on other UK light rail networks.

One key proposal implemented within a year of the disaster was RAIB Recommendation Four, proposing that all UK tram operators, owners and infrastructure managers should work together, 'to research and evaluate systems capable of reliably detecting driver attention state and initiating appropriate

Only 100 yards away from the scene of its 2016 disaster, 2551 pauses at Sandilands on 15 March 2006 as 2550 arrives with a West Croydon service.
(Photo: Gareth Prior)

automatic responses if a low level of alertness is identified.' By October 2017, TfL had fully installed a 'Driver Protection Device' (manufactured by Seeing Machines) which detects and prevents fatigue and distraction. Using safety-verified sensors that track eyelid closures and head movements, when fatigue or distracted behaviour is detected an in-cab alarm is sounded and the driver's seat vibrates to refocus the driver's attention.

Another rapidly-implemented proposal was RAIB Recommendation Five, suggesting that UK tram operators, owners and infrastructure managers, in consultation with the DfT, should work together to review signage, lighting and other visual information for drivers on the approach to high-risk locations such as tight curves. Measures implemented by TfL shortly after the disaster included the adoption of additional speed restrictions and installation of associated signage near Sandilands and at three other locations on the network.

The maximum speed on Tramlink was cut from 80 to 70km/h with enhanced chevron signs installed at four sites with significant bends to provide an additional visual cue for drivers. Other measures adopted for Tramlink include a system called iTram, derived from proven technology on buses, providing drivers with an in-cab speed alert, which was due to have been fitted to all trams by December 2019. Additional temporary lighting has also been installed on the approach to the Sandilands tunnels and, in collaboration with road tunnel lighting experts, a full lighting upgrade of the tunnels was due to have been completed during 2019.

RAIB Recommendations Six, Seven and Eight all relate to the physical characteristics of the tram vehicles, including the strength of windows and doors (Six), ensuring emergency lighting cannot be unintentionally switched off (Seven) and for enabling the rapid evacuation of a tram which is lying on its side after an accident. Action on

these points has included evaluation of alternative glazing options, with the results being shared with UK Trams, and procurement of a lighting system that will operate independently of the tram's battery system in the event of an emergency.

Broader issues regarding the management of tramway operations and risk assessment were covered by RAIB Recommendations Nine and Ten, with the former proposing that the ORR should carry out a review of the regulatory framework for tramways and its long-term strategy for supervision of the sector, and Ten suggesting that TOL and TfL commission an independent review of its process for assessing risk associated with the operation of trams. This independent review was commissioned, with its route risk assessments and risk model shared with the wider UK tram industry, to help inform industry-wide safety standards.

Two recommendations directed specifically at Tramlink operator TOL were that, drawing on expertise from elsewhere in FirstGroup, it should review and, where necessary, improve the management of fatigue risk affecting its tram drivers (Eleven), and that it should commission an external expert or organisation to review the way it learned from operational experiences (Twelve). Responding to the first of these points, TOL engaged a specialist consultancy, implemented a safety improvement plan, and carried out a review of roster-planning, with fatigue management training provided to all staff.

Addressing RAIB Recommendation Twelve, TOL has implemented a 'Just Culture' Programme. This is a long-term project involving significant culture change, through its own internal safety governance arrangements, to address this recommendation. The programme encourages greater communication between colleagues and senior management, while also focusing on customer service and disability awareness training.

2560 at Sandilands Junction on 6 November 2018 with an Elmers End service.

After acknowledgment that earlier reports of excessive speed by trams at the Sandilands junction had produced no response from Tramlink, RAIB Recommendation Thirteen suggested TOL and TfL should improve processes and, where necessary, equipment used for following up both public and employee comments which indicated a possible safety risk. Immediately following the disaster, TfL enhanced its customer complaints process, so that all tram reports were managed by one dedicated TfL team, with any relating to safety prioritised for immediate investigation. Improvements were also made to TfL's website, to make clear where people could make comments, with a specific option to record if a comment related to a safety issue or incident.

Responding to the failure of CCTV monitoring equipment in 2551, which had not been functioning correctly at the time of the disaster, RAIB Recommendation Fourteen said that TfL and TOL should review and, where necessary, improve their processes for inspection and maintaining on-tram CCTV equipment to greatly reduce the likelihood of recorded images being unavailable for accident and incident investigation. Since the disaster the CCTV recording equipment on all Bombardier trams has been replaced and upgraded to digital, bringing it into line with equipment on the newer Stadler trams.

One final RAIB Recommendation (Fifteen) said TOL and TfL should review and, where necessary, revise existing tram maintenance and testing documentation to take account of experience gained and any modification made since the trams were brought into service, and ensure that these documents were kept up-to-date. In response to this, the two parties have undertaken a programme to review and revise their maintenance standards which was scheduled to be completed in 2019.

CHAPTER 10

EXPANDING THE NETWORK

Unlike the tram and light rail networks in Birmingham, Manchester, Nottingham, Tyneside and Sheffield, one feature of Tramlink over the past two decades has been its lack of expansion. Service frequencies have increased as passenger demand has grown, one new stop has opened, Wimbledon station has been expanded and sections of the Wimbledon branch made double track, but the system's overall footprint remains exactly as it was at opening in May 2000.

That is not for lack of interest in its expansion, and right from before its original opening there were a number of ideas for expanding the network to a range of additional destinations. When the House of Commons Transport sub-committee paid a visit to Croydon on

Tramlink and its rail interchanges, as shown in this December 2018 extract from the National Rail London & South East rail service map.

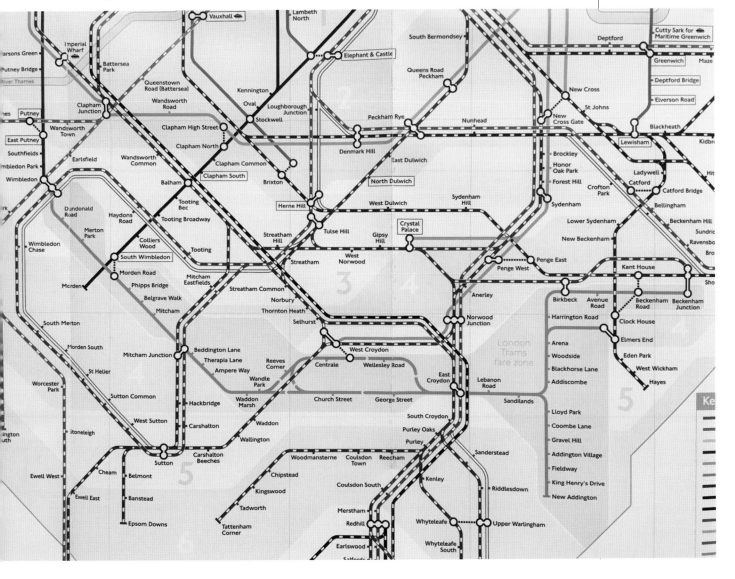

19 January 2000, four months before Tramlink began operations, the committee was told that, 'TCL foresees a number of possible extensions to the original system. Under consideration are a link from Mitcham Junction to Wimbledon via Collier's Wood, and routes to Sutton from the north and the east. Another possibility is an extension to Crystal Palace, which will probably be the first of any new projects.'

Oldest of all plans for extending the network was a spur to Crystal Palace, which would have diverged from the Beckenham Junction line just north of the Harrington Road stop and then run parallel to the single track British Rail route between Beckenham Junction and Crystal Palace. This was very much an ambition of LT's Light Rail director Scott McIntosh during the early development of the system, who told me of his ambition at the time of taking over the BR route, which like Wimbledon–West Croydon was another 'Cinderella' route with a sparse passenger service.

'My long term ambition was to get BR to give up the service from Birkbeck to Crystal Palace, so that instead of just having the rising curve towards Beckenham Junction, you could have a curve in the other direction and run a Crystal Palace to Croydon service,' recalls McIntosh. 'We would have terminated at Crystal Palace Low Level station and would have invested some money in some sort of shallow angle lift, which would have taken you up to the top – rather like what has been done at Ebbw Vale.

'There was a slight problem,' adds the former LT director of Light Rail, 'between Beckenham Junction, where there is a very large railway telephone exchange, and further into Central London there is a tunnel which flooded frequently, and could damage telephone signalling cables, so there were duplicates laid down along the line to Crystal Palace as a telephonic diversionary route for when things went awry.'

Less enthusiastic was another former Tramlink boss, Phil Hewitt: 'Crystal Palace was technically a really challenging project to deliver. It obviously ran alongside and crossed Network Rail, where there were some fairly hefty interfaces that

A December 2017 TfL publicity leaflet heralding planned changes to the Tramlink service pattern including curtailing New Addington services at West Croydon.

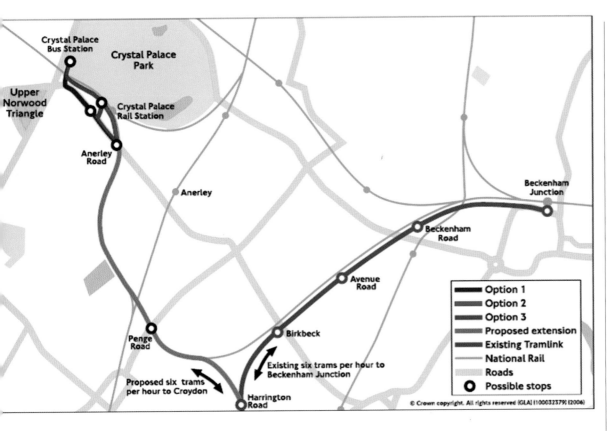

Options for a Tramlink extension to Crystal Palace, as presented in a 2006 consultation exercise by the Greater London Authority.

would have to be managed, and then where it came off the railway alignment it would have a very steep incline up to the terminus in the park [this was assuming services did not simply terminate at the existing low level railway station]. It had a lot of environmental and technical challenges to overcome and a lot of it would have been single line, so from an operational perspective it was always going to be a struggle to get the best out of it.'

A number of options have been examined for taking Tramlink from the former Low Level railway station up to Crystal Palace Parade, where it would have served the existing bus terminus, including both on-street and off-street running. At the time development work was halted, due to lack of funding, the favoured option was for an off-road route that left the railway station and followed the western edge of Crystal Palace Park within the perimeter of the park itself.

While it may have been feasible, and was the first route extension to be considered, one of the criticisms of it

was that it served no obvious point-to-point markets, with existing rail services providing a far more direct Crystal Palace–Croydon journey for those wishing to travel between these two places. However, in looking at Tramlink expansion as part of a 2008 long term review called *Horizon*, Croydon Council identified quite a movement of people from New Addington in the Crystal Palace direction during peak periods.

This review therefore looked into creating a triangular junction at Sandilands, by reinstating a direct north-south rail line in the context of a Crystal Palace extension, with there being just enough room at this tight (and since the 2016 accident, notorious) junction for a 30-metre tram to be able to stand clear of the two existing lines on a single track third-side of the (triangular) junction. This would have allowed the operation of a direct service from Crystal Palace to either New Addington, or simply to Addington Village, if there was insufficient capacity to run a new service all the way to the terminus.

2543 approaches Arena on 6 November 2018 with a Beckenham Junction–Wimbledon service. Trams to Crystal Palace would follow the Beckenham route as far as Harrington Road before diverging to the left shortly beyond the stop.

Birkbeck provides an interchange between Tramlink and Southern rail services on the route from Beckenham Junction to London via Crystal Palace. On 8 November 2018, 455833/812 arrive with the 11.18 to London Bridge.

Trams 2030

Building on the earlier *Horizon* study, in 2016 TfL published a comprehensive vision for development of Tramlink, *Trams for Growth*, to reflect the doubling of passenger numbers since opening, from 14 million a year to 32 million by 2015, and expectations of a near doubling again to 60 million by 2030. This document sets out a 15-year plan to cope with this growth, improve reliability of the system and support regeneration of Croydon town centre, including the new Westfield shopping centre. It looks both at existing upgrade plans, such as the Dingwall Road loop near East Croydon station, and at longer term opportunities for trams in south London.

Summarising the potential for growth in south London, *Trams for Growth* anticipated not only the new shopping centre and other developments in central Croydon placing unprecedented pressure on the tram network, but also enhanced fast rail links from East Croydon to central London and potentially Crossrail Two at Wimbledon driving demand for even more connecting trips on Tramlink. In addition to this, there are plans for mixed-use redevelopment in the Wandle Valley that could include the building of 10-20,000 new homes.

Population growth is a key driver of demand for Tramlink, while Croydon town centre is designated an *Opportunity Area* in the London Plan (a blueprint drawn up in 2016 for development of London over the following 20-25 years) and the focus of growth for the area. These new residents will need local transport to jobs, shops, schools and other facilities, as well as a means of accessing rail links to and from central London. But overcrowding is already a serious problem at peak periods on Tramlink and passenger perceptions of it are formed by their experience of these busy services.

Growth in jobs is principally expected to be in Croydon town centre and at Wimbledon, according to *Trams for Growth*, presenting an opportunity for

A view of the historic Crystal Palace (Low Level) station on 5 April 2019.

A plaque commemorating the station's historic significance.

mode shift from road to light rail as this new employment will be in areas with good public transport. Its 15-year forecast period (2015-30) was also expected to see reducing employment in the Wandle Valley, but the large scale of anticipated residential development could see tram services breathing new life into the

expected mixed-use developments, linking them to the major transport hubs at East Croydon and Wimbledon.

Central Croydon's status as an 'Opportunity Area' in the London Plan means more tram capacity will be needed to cope with the expected development of 7,300 new homes, 280,000 sq m of office space and the 200,000 sq m Westfield shopping centre. At the same time, the study noted that retail and leisure developments were increasingly clustering in bigger centres, making public transport ever more important, including for evening and weekend travel. Trams can help improve access to Croydon and Wimbledon and, with planned extensions, also improve access to Tooting and Sutton.

Tramlink was also identified as having a key role to play in accessing a range of planned and potential enhancements to

Crystal Palace bus station would be the terminus of new Tramlink services. Seen here on 5 April 2019 with the landmark TV transmitter in the background.

the local rail network. These included improved frequencies on the south London metro network, connecting tram users with places like Kingston, Sutton, and Bromley, and completion of the Thameslink programme to give up to sixteen fast trains an hour from East Croydon to central London. In addition, upgrading the Northern Line to Morden and Tooting supported the case for a direct link to Tramlink while, in the longer term, development of Crossrail Two would make Wimbledon an even more important interchange station.

Without the significant investment in Tramlink envisaged in *Trams for Growth*, the existing network and infrastructure would face a host of key challenges by 2030. These included a lack of line capacity across central Croydon for any new services, severe crowding on the Wimbledon branches and through Sandilands on the eastern branches, inadequate depot facilities for any additional trams, and the original 24-strong fleet of Bombardier trams reaching the end of their working lives.

A three phase programme

What *Trams for Growth* describes as its Phase A has already seen work carried out to enhance capacity on the Wimbledon branch, with double tracking between Beddington Lane and Mitcham Junction, together with the creation of an extra platform at Wimbledon, completed in November 2015. What comes next is creation of a new loop line near East Croydon station, known as the Dingwall Loop, which would relieve pressure on the existing town centre route by allowing some services from New Addington to turn using this new loop and so avoid having to use the congested main Croydon loop.

The Dingwall Loop would see trams from New Addington turn right into Dingwall Road after leaving the East Croydon stop, run up to its junction with Lansdowne Road, call at a new stop in Lansdowne Road, then turn left at the junction with Wellesley Road to re-join the main Croydon loop and serve a refurbished Wellesley Road tram stop before returning to East Croydon. Besides giving increased accessibility by public transport to the new Westfield retail scheme, TfL says the loop would allow it to offer a more reliable and resilient service, more trams to New Addington in the short term and an ability to run thirty trams per hour to the east in the long term.

At the time of writing a big question remains over when work on the loop will actually begin, as it is inextricably bound up with progress on the retail scheme. Under the terms of a June 2015 investment submission, by which TfL secured a £5 million contribution from the Greater London Authority (GLA) towards the budgeted £26.81m cost, construction was due to have started in spring 2017, with completion in mid-2019 (later revised to 2020). But delays to the Westfield scheme meant that in June 2018 it was announced that construction would now begin in summer 2019, with completion of the retail development being in spring 2023, and related new homes completed in 2024.

On the basis of its originally budgeted (2015) cost of £26.81m, the bulk of the cost was being met by Westfield (totalling £16.4m) with a smaller contribution of £1.5m from the developers of another scheme, known as Ruskin Square. Crucially, TfL was left to cover any funding gap that arose, either by securing further third-party funding or from its own resources. Only once Westfield construction had begun would an initial £5m of its contribution become payable, with subsequent annual payments of £5m, but until that point TfL was undertaking the project at its own risk and it was estimated that £3m would have been spent in development, consent and procurement before the first Westfield contribution was received.

A 2016 TfL plan of central Croydon. The Dingwall Road loop (or eastern turn-back as it is now known) would run up Dingwall Road just west of East Croydon station, turn left into Lansdowne Road, then re-join the existing route close to the Wellesley Road stop.

A view looking north along Dingwall Road on 5 April 2019 – trams would run along the left-hand side of the road before turning left into Lansdowne Road at the roundabout.

Enhancing the Wandle Valley
(Trams for Growth Phase B)

On a significantly grander scale than the Dingwall Loop are ambitions in the *Trams for Growth* strategy to develop the Croydon to Wimbledon corridor. Here the document identifies the potential for vast new residential developments, with up to 10,000 new homes in what it calls Wandle Valley East, an area stretching from the west side of Croydon to roughly the Therapia Lane tram stop. It then suggests potential for up to another 10,000 homes in Wandle Valley West, the area north-west of Therapia Lane and extending to the Beddington Lane tram stop.

Tramlink would have a key role to play, by linking these huge new developments with local transport hubs at Mitcham Junction, South Wimbledon and West Croydon, where there is the potential for better interchange and more frequent connecting services. This is in addition to the major enhancements at the two strategic transport hubs – Wimbledon and East Croydon – through Thameslink and Crossrail Two, enabling frequent and easy access to Central London for the new Wandle Valley communities.

To unlock this vast potential would require major changes to planning policies on the part of the GLA and the local councils in Croydon and Sutton, but if such a scale of development was to go ahead, the 'planning gain' from granting consent to major new house-building could be used to fund many of the tram enhancements that would be needed. These would include relieving remaining bottlenecks – single track sections on the Wimbledon branch at Phipps Bridge and the Wandle Park Flyover in Croydon – as well as construction of a new spur from Phipps Bridge to connect with the upgraded Northern Line at South Wimbledon.

The once 'Cinderella' Wimbledon–Croydon rail route has the potential to become the backbone of this development corridor and, if existing bottlenecks could be eliminated, then frequencies could be almost doubled from 12 trams per hour (tph) to 23 tph, while a South Wimbledon spur would create an important new destination at the western end of the line, improving local connectivity to the Wandle Valley. A number of further enhancements would be needed to deliver this scale of service however, including a new 'turnback' in central Croydon, more vehicles, additional depot facilities, and power supply upgrades.

Opening of a short spur to South Wimbledon would relieve a potential bottleneck at Wimbledon which, even with the additional Tramlink platform that was added in 2015, can only handle a maximum of 15 tph until more platform capacity is eventually freed up by the opening of Crossrail Two, when many suburban services would be diverted to serve a new underground station. Such a spur would allow for increased frequencies along the Wandle Valley, support potential development of more housing in the South Wimbledon and Colliers Wood areas, and also provide a northern terminus for a potential extension of Tramlink southwards to Sutton.

Sutton has long been talked about as a logical extension of Tramlink and, in July 2013, London Mayor Boris Johnson declared that there was a reasonable business case for Tramlink to cover the Wimbledon–Sutton corridor. A map has been released showing the planned route. It would leave the existing tramway just to the east of Morden Road and head along the A24 and A297 to Rosehill Roundabout, then the B2230 through Sutton town centre, ending at the rail station.

Trams for Growth put an estimated price tag of £320m (2016 price) on an 8km-long scheme. This would also include the link to South Wimbledon tube station and run in a southerly direction from close to the existing Morden Road tram stop, with up

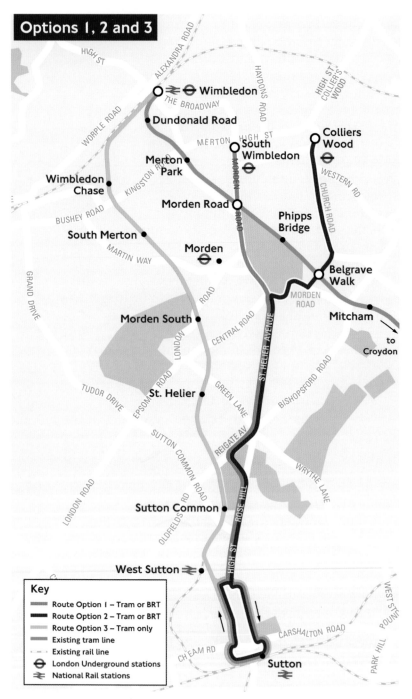

Options 1, 2 and 3

Key

▬▬	Route Option 1 – Tram or BRT
▬▬	Route Option 2 – Tram or BRT
▬▬	Route Option 3 – Tram only
▬▬	Existing tram line
⋯⋯	Existing rail line
⊖	London Underground stations
⇌	National Rail stations

A TfL map showing three alternative routes to Sutton that were put forward in the 2018 consultation exercise.

A public consultation on the Sutton Link

As with virtually every other rail-related infrastructure scheme, the estimated cost of a road-based Tramlink extension to Sutton had soared to £425m by the time a public consultation exercise was launched in October 2018. This included the proposed 2016 alignment, along with two alternatives, one using the existing heavy rail route (costing £300m), and a lower cost alternative (£275m) using a system called bus rapid transit (BRT) instead of light rail on the two proposed road-based alignments. In a preamble to its consultation, TfL said a Sutton link would open up transport options for communities that could include St Helier, Rosehill and north Sutton, which are not presently served by high-capacity public transport.

In addition to this, the link would create or improve connections to other centres, which could include Wimbledon, South Wimbledon or Colliers Wood, with links to London Underground and National Rail services. It would also make it much easier to travel by public transport to key locations along the route, which could include several schools, the open spaces of Rosehill Park and Morden Hall Park, St Helier Hospital, and potentially the London Cancer Hub being planned for Belmont, via a future extension which would be enabled by the Sutton Link. It would also make roads safer and more attractive for people walking, cycling and using public transport.

TfL pointed out that a new link would support development of Sutton town centre, where there are plans to create up to 5,000 homes and 2,000 new jobs by 2031, along with better public spaces and environments for walking and cycling. It would support plans for Morden town centre, which aim to make it much more attractive for locals, workers and visitors to enjoy and to provide up to 1,800 new homes in the centre. At present parts of both boroughs (Sutton and Merton) have very limited public transport options and

to a dozen new stops, including one within walking distance of Morden tube station and a potential loop to serve St Helier Hospital, with services terminating at Sutton railway station. There is strong local support for such a new route, with potential for more housing growth along it.

the Sutton Link would help enable the delivery of new homes and jobs in these areas, added TfL.

The 2018 consultation followed an earlier exercise in 2014, when the London boroughs of Sutton and Merton, supported by TfL, had held a public consultation on a proposed extension to Tramlink from Wimbledon to Sutton. The results of that exercise had demonstrated strong backing for the proposed tram extension with 84% of over 10,000 respondents supporting it. Building on this work, Mayor Sadiq Khan instructed TfL to continue evaluation of opportunities for an extension to Sutton.

As part of this process, TfL's investigation included a full range of alternatives that could bring similar benefits, hence the consideration of

bus rapid transit(BRT) as well as light rail. Having whittled down more than 180 options to the three being presented for public consultation, TfL indicated that Option 1 (the previously published alignment to South Wimbledon tube station) or Option 2 (a variant following Morden Road towards the Belgrave Walk tram stop and then continuing along Church Road to Colliers Wood tube station) best achieved its aims. Option 3 (use of the existing railway) was regarded as the least suitable means of improving public transport within Merton and Sutton. It would also need to be closely coordinated with the proposed Crossrail Two station in Wimbledon to minimise disruption to Wimbledon town centre, and so could delay delivery of a Sutton Link by several years.

Sutton is another busy rail interchange, which Tramlink would serve at street level, seen here on 5 April 2019

Summing up arguments in favour of Option 1 – the street-based route with interchanges at Morden Road for Tramlink and South Wimbledon for the Northern Line – TfL said it would deliver a quick journey time of around 19 minutes between South Wimbledon and Sutton town centre compared to 35 minutes today; serve both Morden and Sutton town centres effectively, improving public transport access to existing communities and new developments; provide an interchange at Sutton railway station; improve public transport to less well served areas such as St Helier Avenue, Rosehill, Angel Hill and Sutton North; and have potential to connect directly with the existing tram network.

Arguments against Option 1 were that it would be challenging to construct a connection to the existing London Trams network at Morden Road (assuming a tram extension rather than a BRT service); some negative impacts on parks and open space at Rosehill Park West and Nelson Gardens; impact on certain commercial properties in Morden Road; and disruption to road and bus users during construction. It would also be difficult to provide a direct tram service from Sutton to Wimbledon station, because of difficulty of construction at Morden Road tram stop, while priority at junctions for tram or BRT services would result in longer journey times for some road users.

Looking at Option 2 – the alternative street-based route from Colliers Wood to Sutton town centre with a Tramlink interchange at Belgrave Walk tram stop and the Northern line at Colliers Wood – TfL again said that this would speed up journey times (to around 21 minutes between Colliers Wood and Sutton town centre compared to 37 minutes today). There would be fewer engineering constraints in connecting to the existing Tramlink network at Belgrave Walk (if delivered as a tram extension) and this would be the most effective option for improving the public transport network in less well connected areas, such as Belgrave

Walk, while also improving public transport at St Helier Avenue, Rosehill, Angel Hill and Sutton North.

Arguments against Option 2 were that it gave no direct access to Morden town centre (an approximately 800 metre walk); there would be less opportunity to separate vehicles from general traffic (particularly along Morden Road and Church Road); some negative impacts on open space in Rosehill Park West; and it was likely to affect more commercial properties than other options, primarily at Belgrave Walk. As with Option 1, there would also be disruption to road and bus users during construction and priority at junctions for tram or BRT services would result in longer journey times for some road users.

Both Options 1 and 2 would have the potential for a loop to serve St Helier Hospital directly, as previously featured in the *Trams for Growth* proposals, but more work would be required to explore whether this could be provided. While both options could be provided by the lower cost bus rapid transit alternative to trams, TfL warns that the cost of operating and maintaining a BRT service is expected to be higher than for a tram service, particularly because more vehicles and drivers are required to provide the more frequent service required.

Option 3 would see trams replace trains on the existing Sutton Loop railway line, providing interchange at Wimbledon with Tramlink, National Rail and London Underground's District Line. This would mean more frequent and accessible services at existing stations on the Sutton Loop (Wimbledon Chase, South Merton, Morden South, St. Helier and Sutton Common). It would make least use of roads – the only on-street section being in Sutton town centre – so have least impact on road users as well as less negative impact on existing open space, trees and property. Downsides of Option 3 were that it did not deliver significant journey time improvements, would mean the loss of existing Thameslink rail services on the Sutton Loop line, no interchange with the Northern Line, and would require extensive work at Wimbledon station.

Longer term expansion plans (Trams for Growth Phase C)

Earlier studies into expansion of Tramlink's footprint have looked beyond merely taking the system to Crystal Palace and at a host of other possible destinations. These have included the busy bus corridor from Purley, to the south of Croydon and Streatham to its north, much of which would be on a shared alignment with existing trunk roads. Such a route could have included a park-and-ride site close to the M23 motorway and a rail interchange at Streatham. Other studies that have not been progressed looked at links to a range of other significant south London locations, including Biggin Hill, Bromley and Lewisham.

The 2016 blueprint for expanding Tramlink was costed at £737m (2016 prices), representing an investment averaging £43m/year over around 15 years. How this would be funded remains uncertain, but the strategy document notes that £92m is already committed, and that in a scenario where 20,000 new homes are created, a notional levy of £10,000 per home would generate a further £200m. In addition to this, a proposed development area known as the Croydon Growth Zone could generate up to a further £50m.

Looking beyond the first two stages of the strategy – the Dingwall Loop (now officially known as the 'eastern turn-back') enhanced services to New Addington and along the Wandle Valley, and the Sutton extension – a third phase to the plan would see double tracking of the remaining single line sections on the Wimbledon route, a new passing loop or double tracking on the Beckenham branch, expansion to the existing Therapia Lane depot, and development of additional depot facilities, probably in the Elmers End area. Longer trams are one other option for increasing capacity, but this would be a very costly option requiring platform extensions at every stop.

Summing up its vision for trams, TfL says it is to support more jobs and homes in south London, connect people into fast links to central London and be part of a more frequent local rail network. Adopting *Trams for Growth* in full would enable delivery of 20,000 new homes, reduce waiting times to no more than ten minutes and in most cases no more than four minutes, achieve an 88% increase in overall frequency and a 180% increase in capacity on the Wimbledon branch, 88% more frequency and capacity to New Addington, and 25% more frequency and 88% more capacity on the Beckenham Junction branch.

BIBLIOGRAPHY

Little has been published on Tramlink since its opening in 2000 so much of this book has been based on formal documents published during the evaluation, appraisal of options and tendering processes.

I am particularly indebted to Nico Dekker, Director of Rail Systems Consultants Ltd, for the opportunity to study an extensive range of original documents relating to development of Tramlink.

As mentioned elsewhere in this book, Nico has held a number of roles in the system's development, and documents from his formidable archive are highlighted with an asterisk (*) in the list below. For ease of reference these original sources are ranked in chronological rather than in alphabetical order:

Light Rail: Some Implications for the South East* - London and South East Regional Planning Conference (Serplan), David Hurdle, December 1988

Light Rail for Beginners: A One Day Symposium* - LB Croydon (notes of proceedings), Fairfield Halls, Croydon, 28 November 1990

Croydon Light Rail (Tramlink)* – Report considered by the LB Croydon Highways & Transportation, Planning and Resources, Finance & Policy Committees, 27 February 1991

Tramlink: Light Rail in Croydon* - LB Croydon, April 1991

Tramlink: Report on Schemes for Consideration at Public Consultation* - G. Maunsell/MVA for London Transport/ LB Croydon, April 1991

Croydon Tramlink – Environmental Statement* - Halcrow Fox, November 1991

Croydon Tramlink – Initial Review of System* - GEC Alstom (for LB Croydon), April 1992

Croydon Tramlink – Outline Performance Specification* - June 1992

Croydon Tramlink Bill (as amended in committee)* - 1993

Parliamentary Debates (Hansard) – Croydon Tramlink Bill (second reading) 21 July 1993 (Vol 229, no. 221, columns 406-43)

Urban Improvement Proposals* – Segesta (architects, Barcelona), December 1993

Tramlink Overhead Line System Study – Final Report* - Railway Systems Consultants/MPB Ltd/Design Triangle, London Borough of Croydon, November 1993

Tramlink Tramstop Review for the London Borough of Croydon* – Globe Architects (Sheffield)/Plan Design Group (Halifax), January 1994

Croydon Tramlink – System Description, Base Scheme* – Project Development Group, 10 February 1994

Croydon Tramlink Section 56 Submission (draft)* - London Transport, 4 March 1994

Croydon Tramlink Act, 21 July 1994

Interim Feasibility Proposals – East Croydon Station Tramlink Stop* - Alan Brookes Associates (architects), July 1994

Proforma Performance Specification* – [Tramlink] Project Development Group, 1995

Croydon Tramlink – Demand Update (Summary Report)* - MVA Consultancy for London Transport, September 1995

Instructions to Tenderers (draft)* – Freshfields, 8 September 1995

Further Information for Tenderers* - Freshfields, 1995

Invitation and Procedures Letter* - London Transport/LB Croydon, 1995

Tramlink Information Memorandum* - London Transport/LB Croydon, 1995

Off-tram revenue agreement* – London Regional Transport, 1995

Selection of Tenderers* - London Transport/LB Croydon, 15 September 1995

Tramlink General Agreement* - LB Croydon, 1995

Tramlink Context Studies* (route plans) – LB Croydon, September 1995

Croydon Tramlink Overhead Line Study – Part II of II* - Railway Systems Consultants, London Borough of Croydon, November 1995

Tender Submission for Croydon Tramlink Enabling Works, Volume 1* - Railtrack, 6 November 1995

London De Luxe AZ Atlas – Geographers' A-Z Map Company, 1998

Tramlink – Official Handbook, Michael Steward, Jon Gent, Colin Stannard, Capital Transport, 2000

Tramlink User Guide - (pre-launch publicity leaflet), 2000

Croydon Tramlink Impact Study (summary of the main findings) - Transport for London, June 2002

Amey plc – Annual Report & Accounts 2002 (as filed at Companies House)

Croydon Tramways – Robert J. Harley, Capital Transport, 2004

Integrated Transport: the future of light rail and modern trams in Britain – memorandum to the House of Commons Select Committee on Transport by Roger Harding, General Manager TCL, February 2005

Tramlink Operations – A paper presented to the Transport for London Rail and Underground Panel on 12 July 2011 by Phil Hewitt, Director, London Tramlink

Dingwall Road Loop, Croydon – Paper presented to the Greater London Authority's Investment & Performance Board on 17 June 2015

London Trams: User Guide - Mayor of London/Transport for London, April 2016

Trams for Growth – A TfL presentation on enhancing the network, April 2016

Rail (magazine) – Issues 821 (1 March 2017); 842 (20 December 2017); 843 (3 January 2018) – reports and features on the 2016 Sandilands disaster

britishtramsonline.co.uk – an excellent and comprehensive enthusiast website, with extensive coverage of Tramlink and every other British tram system

croydon-tramlink.co.uk – the unofficial site by Stephen Parascandalo – lots of detailed background on the early years of Tramlink (to 2008)

Evening Standard – Reports following the 2016 Sandilands disaster: 'Lessons must be learned from Croydon' (9 November 2017); 'Croydon: an accident waiting to happen' (7 December 2017)

The Times/Sunday Times – Reports on the 2016 Sandilands disaster: 'Tram driver arrested after seven die in rush hour crash' (10 November 2016); 'Tram drivers feared "nasty bend"' (*The Sunday Times* – 13 November 2016); 'Tram in fatal crash was doing 43mph round 12mph bend (17 November 2016); 'Tram safety fears as four drivers admit falling asleep at controls' (25 April 2017)

Rail Accident Investigation Branch (RAIB) – Reports on Tramlink incidents: Derailments at Phipps Bridge (21/10/05 and 25/05/06); Collision at New Addington (23/11/05); Incident at Wellesley Road (15/07/07); Fatal accident at Morden Hall (13/09/08); Derailment of tram at East Croydon (17/02/12); Pedestrian struck by tram at Sandilands (16/05/12); Tram running with doors open (13/04/13); Overturning of tram at Sandilands Junction (09/11/16 – updated report)

Transport for London (TfL) – Progress update on RAIB recommendations (following 2016 Sandilands disaster) – November 2018

ACKNOWLEDGMENTS

I would like to thank a number of individuals who have been willing to share their first-hand experience of Tramlink with me, and so helped bring alive the fascinating story of its development and subsequent growth.

Particular thanks go to Nico Dekker, John Dolan, Phil Hewitt, Scott McIntosh, John Rymer, Jim Snowdon and Frank Wilton. Sincere thanks also to David Edwards in the press office at TfL for organising and hosting a visit for me to Therapia Lane depot on 16 January 2019.

I would also like to thank 'the Voice of Tramlink' – former ITN newsreader Nicholas Owen – for kindly agreeing to write a foreword to this story, as he did in the *Official Tramlink Handbook*, published in 2000.

For early pictures of Tramlink I am hugely grateful to the family of Stephen Parascandalo for allowing me to reproduce photos from his marvellous website, and also to Gareth Prior of the excellent and highly-recommended tram enthusiast website britishtramsonline.co.uk for other pre-2008 photos of trams in their original red and white livery.

INDEX

Points position indicators (PPIs) 92
Private Finance Initiative (PFI) 10, 17, 40,
    58, 62-4, 77-9, 83-5, 90, 95, 107
Project Development Group (PDG) 10,
    40-1, 43, 46, 49, 51-2, 55-9
Project Seagull 105, 107
Purley Way 12, 65, 139, 162

Rail Accident Investigation Branch (RAIB)
    10, 92, 110, 113, 165-71, 173-80
Rail Business Intelligence (magazine) 109
Rail Systems Consultants (RSC) 57
Railway Inspectorate (HMRI) 10, 56,
    90, 109
Reagan, Matthew 107
Reeves Corner 113, 139-41, 143, 160, 162
Ridley, Nicholas MP 147
Road Traffic Accident (RTA) 10, 159-60
Royal Bank of Scotland 59, 78
Runnacles, Tim 14
Rymer, John 10, 74

St. Helier 190, 192
St. Martin's Property Corporation 82
Sanderstead 12, 24-5, 28, 30, 33, 39,
    149, 153
Sandilands 28, 30, 38, 43, 56, 59, 61, 82-3,
    89, 95, 114, 144-6, 153, 159-62, 165,
    169-75, 178-80, 183, 187
Sheffield Supertram 62
Shirley Woods 13
Smith, Howard 110, 121
Snowdon, Jim 10, 111
South East Regional Planning Conference
    (Serplan) 19
South London Partnership 75
South Norwood Country Park 23, 33-6, 48,
    147, 149
South Wimbledon 189-92
Special purpose vehicles (SPVs) 77
Stadler 10, 11, 64, 117-8, 121, 123, 128, 131,
    154, 170, 180
Strzelecki, Mike 15
Sunday Times, The 172
Surrey Iron Railway 18, 25
Sutton 27-8, 48, 61, 74, 139, 182, 186-93

Tamworth Road (see Centrale)
Tarmac 10, 40, 42-3, 55, 59
Teevan Close 30, 34, 147
Thameslink 13, 17, 45, 130, 187, 189, 193

Therapia Lane 7, 28, 34-6, 55, 63, 65, 69, 71,
    73-4, 81, 114-5, 117, 119, 121, 127-9, 137,
    159-60, 189, 193
Thompson, Sharon 121, 124
Ticket machines 58, 60, 66, 81, 89, 113,
    125-6, 131, 157
Times, The 78, 172-3
Townsend, Jackie 10
Tramlink Liaison Committee 17
Tram Operations Limited (TOL) 9-11, 128,
    169-70, 172, 176
Trams for Growth (TfL 2016 study) 185,
    187, 189, 192-3
Tramtrack Croydon Limited (TCL) 9-11,
    59-61, 64-7, 71, 73-4, 76-93, 95, 105-12,
    115, 162-4, 182
Tramways and Urban Transit
    (magazine) 120
Tramways Act 1870 37
Transdev 10, 11, 40, 42
Transport and General Workers' Union
    (TGWU) 73
Transport Act (1968) – Section 56 10, 43,
    51-2, 54
Transport for London (TfL) 9-11, 30, 46,
    60-1, 71, 73-4, 76-95, 105-12, 115,
    162-4, 182
Travelcard 11, 52, 54, 69, 80, 84, 95, 126
Turner & Townsend (T&T) 11, 62

Vandalism 66, 108, 160, 162
Variobahn 10, 11, 64, 118-9, 154

Waddon Marsh 28-9, 65-6, 138-9
Wandle Park 27, 35, 44, 65, 88, 118, 139,
    177, 189
Wandle Valley 12-3, 137, 185-6, 189, 193
Webster, Richard 107
Wellesley Road 17, 27, 67, 82, 101, 112-3,
    128, 141-3, 160, 164, 187-8
West Croydon 13-4, 17-8, 21, 24-7, 32-3, 37,
    52, 54, 58, 66, 68-9, 121, 123, 126, 133, 139,
    141-4, 162, 182, 189
Westfield 185-7
Whitgift Shopping Centre 71-2
Wicks, Malcolm MP 50
Wimbledon 8, 12-4, 17, 21, 25, 27-8, 31-3,
    37-8, 47-8, 51, 55, 58, 60-3, 66-7, 69, 72-3,
    77, 81-2, 108, 113-7, 122-34, 137, 141,
    143-4, 161, 165, 181-2, 185-7, 189-93
Woodside 25, 30, 33, 35, 39, 79, 147-8